Keto PowerXL Grill Air Fryer Combo Cookbook

600-Day Delicious and Healthy Low-Carbs Recipes to Fry, Bake, Grill, and Roast with Your PowerXL Grill Air Fryer Combo

Tirder Wuckey

© Copyright 2021 Tirder Wuckey - All Rights Reserved.

In no way is it legal to reproduce, duplicate, or transmit any part of this document by either electronic means or in printed format. Recording of this publication is strictly prohibited, and any storage of this material is not allowed unless with written permission from the publisher. All rights reserved.

The information provided herein is stated to be truthful and consistent, in that any liability, regarding inattention or otherwise, by any usage or abuse of any policies, processes, or directions contained within is the solitary and complete responsibility of the recipient reader. Under no circumstances will any legal liability or blame be held against the publisher for any reparation, damages, or monetary loss due to the information herein, either directly or indirectly.

Respective authors own all copyrights not held by the publisher.

Legal Notice:

This book is copyright protected. This is only for personal use. You cannot amend, distribute, sell, use, quote or paraphrase any part of the content within this book without the consent of the author or copyright owner. Legal action will be pursued if this is breached.

Disclaimer Notice:

Please note the information contained within this document is for educational and entertainment purposes only. Every attempt has been made to provide accurate, up-to-date and reliable, complete information. No warranties of any kind are expressed or implied. Readers acknowledge that the author is not engaging in the rendering of legal, financial, medical or professional advice.

By reading this document, the reader agrees that under no circumstances are we responsible for any losses, direct or indirect, which are incurred as a result of the use of information contained within this document, including, but not limited to, errors, omissions, or inaccuracies.

Table of Contents

Introduction.. 6
Chapter 1: The Basics of Keto Diet.. 7
    What is Keto Diet?.. 7
    How does Keto Diet Work?... 7
    How to Know Whether Your Body is in Ketosis or Not?................. 7
    The Advantages of Keto Diet... 9
    Tips and Tricks for Successful Keto Journey................................... 10
Chapter 2: The Basics of PowerXL Grill Air Fryer Combo.......................... 12
    What is PowerXL Grill Air Fryer Combo?.. 12
    Parts and Accessories.. 12
    Operating Buttons and Preset Functions... 14
    Cleaning and Maintenance.. 15
Chapter 3: Breakfast.. 17
    Almond Butter Oatmeal..................................
    Nutritious Zucchini Muffins..................................
    Healthy Spinach Frittata..................................
    Artichoke Mushroom Quiche..................................
    Delicious Jalapeno Bread..................................
    Blueberry Oatmeal..................................
    Healthy Spinach Frittata..................................
    Healthy Kale Zucchini Bake..................................
    Delicious Berry Oatmeal..................................
    Healthy Oat Breakfast Muffins..................................
Chapter 4: Poultry... 27
    Chicken Shawarma..................................
    Mexican Chicken Lasagna..................................
    Roasted Pepper Chicken..................................
    Delicious Tandoori Chicken..................................
    Chicken Paillard..................................
    Easy Slow Cook Chicken..................................
    Chicken Fajita Casserole..................................
    Spicy Chicken Ginger Soup..................................
    Greek Tomato Olive Chicken..................................
    Broccoli Chicken Casserole..................................
    Apple Chicken..................................
    Baked Chicken Mushrooms..................................
    Honey Mustard Chicken..................................
    Meatballs..................................
    Simple & Easy Slow Cook Chicken..................................
    Chicken with Artichoke Hearts..................................
    Tender & Juicy Chicken..................................
    Chicken Cacciatore..................................
    Greek Chicken..................................
    Asian Chicken Wings..................................
    Tasty Caribbean Chicken..................................
    Ranch Chicken..................................
    Crispy Crusted Chicken..................................
    Caesar Chicken..................................
    Chili Garlic Chicken Wings..................................
Chapter 5: Beef, Pork & Lamb.. 52

 Meatballs.................................
 Italian Beef Roast........................
 Italian Pork Roast........................
 Shredded Beef............................
 Greek Pork Chops........................
 Delicious Mongolian Beef...............
 Beef Fajitas...............................
 Salsa Pork Chops.........................
 Flavorful Steak Fajitas...................
 Delicious Beef Stroganoff...............
 Beef with Potatoes........................
 Beef Ragu..................................
 Moist Pork Roast.........................

 Tender & Moist Lamb Roast...............
 Jalapeno Beef..............................
 Juicy Pork Tenderloin.....................
 Dijon Pork Chops.........................
 Meatballs..................................
 Pork Chop Cacciatore....................
 Lamb Patties..............................
 Tasty Flank Steak.........................
 Curried Pork Chops......................
 Flavorful Beef Curry......................
 Beef Bean Chili...........................
 Flavorful Beef Chili.......................

Chapter 6: Fish & Seafood..77
 Lime Cajun Salmon......................
 Salmon Casserole........................
 Lime Garlic Cod..........................
 Greek Salmon.............................
 Scallop Gratin.............................
 Sweet Orange Salmon...................
 Lemon Pepper Basa.....................
 Buttery Scallops..........................

 Delicious Pesto Salmon..................
 Baked Catfish.............................
 Italian Halibut.............................
 Sweet & Spicy Cajun Salmon..........
 Dijon Salmon.............................
 Baked Shrimp............................
 Dill White Fish Fillets...................

Chapter 7: Vegetables & Side Dishes..92
 Healthy Artichoke Casserole...........
 Baked Cauliflower........................
 Red Beans Rice...........................
 Delicious Carrot Tomato Soup........
 Flavorful Ratatouille.....................
 Curried Tomato Soup...................
 Three Bean Chili.........................
 Tomato Green Bean Soup.............
 Creamy Cauliflower Casserole........
 Stuffed Pepper...........................

 Baked Eggplant & Zucchini...........
 Mushroom Barley Soup................
 Easy Baked Beans........................
 Scalloped Potatoes.......................
 Mac & Cheese............................
 Healthy Broccoli Casserole............
 Baked Tomato............................
 Slow Cooked Vegetables................
 Barley Risotto............................
 Bean Stew.................................

Chapter 8: Snacks & Appetizers...112
 Sweet Potato Bites.......................

 Tofu Bites..................................

    Veggie Fritters..
    Spinach Dip..
    Healthy Taro Fries...................................
    Easy Cauliflower Bites............................
    Delicious Cheese Dip...............................
    Flavorful Chicken Dip..............................
    Healthy Tofu Fries....................................

    Crispy & Flavorful Okra..
    Spicy Spinach Dip...
    Ricotta Dip..
    Healthy Carrot Fries..
    Easy Stuffed Mushrooms..
    Chicken Stuffed Peppers..

Chapter 9: Desserts..127
    Moist Lemon Cake....................................
    Almond Date Brownies...........................
    Coconut Carrot Cake................................
    Blueberry Carrot Bars..............................
    Yummy Strawberry Cobbler..................

    Delicious Peanut Butter Brownie............................
    Delicious Peanut Butter Cake..................................
    Chewy Brownies...
    Cinnamon Apple Slices..
    Simple & Easy Yogurt Cake....................................

Chapter 10: 30-Day Meal Plan...137
Conclusion...140

Introduction

Do you want to revolutionize your cooking experience with a multifunctional cooking appliance? Do you want to go on a keto diet? Overall, a long term ketogenic diet can help reduce your risk of diabetes, heart disease, stroke, Alzheimer's and other conditions in your daily life. If you answer yes to any of these questions, please relax and read further to know more about it. The Keto PowerXL Grill Air Fryer Combo Cookbook is definitely a perfect solution to you.

Over the years, the PowerXL has been designing and creating quality products that cater to the needs of consumers worldwide. They never fail to reach that. After so many years, they are still going strong. Their vision is to produce quality products that will keep up with modern trends and consumer demand, which is why we consider them a front runner in the appliance industry today.

The Keto PowerXL Grill Air Fryer Combo Cookbook will change the way you cook in the kitchen. If you want to grill, rotisserie, roast, toast, air fry or even bake pizza, then this appliance will help you do that. It allows you to have your desired outcome without compromising on the taste and flavor of your food. Its versatility is what makes it stand out from the rest of its competitors in the market.

You can grill all your preferred meat meals with just a few minutes. It uses infrared heat to cook your food in a convenient and healthy way. Processed food is not good for the body. But with the PowerXL Grill Air Fryer, you don't have to worry about that anymore because it allows you to prepare raw meat perfectly. You can even add some vegetables and they will be cooked in no time at all. The more you promote healthy eating habits in the family, the more chances of living a longer and healthier life. This cookbook has all that you need to get started keto diet with the PowerXL Grill Air Fryer and make your life in the kitchen better.

Chapter 1: The Basics of Keto Diet

What is Keto Diet?

The Keto diet is one of the most effective and popular diet plans comes with long term health benefits. Keto is a low-carb, high-fat diet plan that allows a moderate amount of protein during the diet period. Keto is not just a diet plan it completely changes your daily food eating habit towards natural and healthy food consumption. Generally, our body depends on glucose (carb) for energy to perform day-to-day activities. When the glucose level in our body increases the excess glucose is converted into glycogens and stored in liver and body cells.

The Keto diet is a low carb diet, so the carb consumption is reduced during a keto diet. Due to this glucose level is decreased and our body finds out the alternative source for energy. It breaks down fats for energy. This state of the body is also called ketosis. It is one of the metabolic processes where fats are broken down and produce ketones for energy. These ketones provide an endless source of energy to our body. The Keto diet is one of the most followed diets for weight loss purposes. It not only maintains your healthy body weight but also improves your physical and mental health.

How does Keto Diet Work?

In general, our body uses glucose (carb) as a primary source of energy. When we reduce the intake of carbohydrates during the diet, glucose level automatically reduces. In this condition, our body shifts itself to break down fats for energy in the absence of carbohydrates (glucose). In fat breaking process some fatty acids are released our livers convert these fatty acids into ketones.

Ketones are produced due to a chemical process when our body burns fat for energy instead of glucose. Most of the body organs and tissues use these ketones as an alternative source of energy. Ketones are one of the best fuels for our brain they fulfill more than 70% of our brain energy needs. The lack of glucose pushes our body into the state of ketosis.

How to Know Whether Your Body is in Ketosis or Not?

There are several sign and symptoms and methods which indicate that your body is in the state of ketosis or not. These signs, symptoms, and methods are mention as follows.

- **Increase in thirst and dry mouth**

This is one of the common side effects noticed when you are following a keto diet. In this state, your body loses excess sodium and water, so it is recommended that add 2 to 4 grams of sodium into your diet to balancing the electrolyte level into your body. This will also increase the urination process and increase thirst. These signs and symptoms indicate that your body is in a state of ketosis.

- **Keto Breath or Bad Breath**

This is one of the common side effects noticed during the first week of the keto diet. When your body breaks down fats for energy, in this process acetone are release and produce a fruity smell or nail polish remover like smell having the bad breath symptoms. This is happening due to keto diet plan adaptation. Keto breath or bad breath symptoms will indicate that your body is in the state of ketosis.

- **Rapid Weight Loss**

This happens when your body breaks down fats for energy instead of glucose (carb). If you notice that your weight is rapidly reduced during the first week of the keto diet, then. Rapid weight loss is another sign and symptom that indicates that your body is in the state of ketosis.

- **Blood Test**

A blood test is one of the common and accurate methods used to measure the ketones level. It is one of the few expensive methods of measuring blood ketones levels in diabetic patients. The blood test method is similar to a glucometer test. In this case, you need to use a keto meter instead of a glucometer with a lancet pen and test strips. If the keto meter shows reading 0.5 and 3 mml/L which indicates that your body is in the state of ketosis.

- **Ketostix**

Ketostix is one of the accurate and inexpensive ways to check your ketones level in the urine. You just need to collect the urine in a clean urine container then dip the Ketostix and shake to remove the excess urine from the stick and wait for 15 seconds. After 15 minutes you have noticed that Ketostix color is changed. To measure the ketones level just follow the color guide match with your strip color to check the ketosis.

- **Increase focus and energy**

Most people notice that tiredness and sickness during the first few days of the keto diet. When your body uses ketones for energy. It not only improves your physical health but also improves your focus and energy. This is happening because 70% of brain energy needs are fulfilled by ketones. This is another sign which indicates that your body is in the state of ketosis.

The Advantages of Keto Diet

The keto diet is one of the most popular diets for years comes with various kinds of health benefits some of them are described as follows.

- **Rapid Weight loss**

If you are overweight and want to reduce the extra weight rapidly then the keto diet is one of the best choices to maintain your healthy body weight. During the keto diet, our body breaks down fats for energy instead of glucose. Due to this fat breaking process, you have notice rapid weight loss. The diet allows a moderate number of proteins, so you don't feel hungrier during the diet period. This will help to reduce your bodyweight rapidly and gives you long term weight loss benefits.

- **Improve your Brain Functions**

Keto diet is low carb diet, due to low carb consumption glucose level decreases and our body finds out alternative energy source by breaking the fats for energy. During the fat breaking process some chemical releases. Our liver converts these chemicals into ketones. To perform day-to-day operations our body use ketones as an energy source. It fulfills more than 70% of brain energy needs. Most of the study and research proves that ketones improve focus, attention and memory functions.

- **Effective on various medical conditions**

The keto diet is not only used for weight loss purposes but also used to treat various medical conditions like Alzheimer's, Parkinson's, type-2 diabetes, heart-related disease, blood pressure, and also in epilepsy conditions.

- Improves Cholesterol Levels

The keto diet is a low-carb high-fat diet. It allows you to consume healthy fats during the diet period. Healthy fats are responsible to improve the HDL (good cholesterol) level. Carbohydrates are one of the main reasons to increase the LDL (bad cholesterol) level. The Keto diet is a low-carb diet, so it decreases the LDL level and also reduces the risk of heart-related disease.

- Control Appetite

The keto diet is a low carb, high fat, and moderate protein diet. The diet is enriching with all essential nutrients the moderate protein in diet which helps prevent an increase in appetite. You never feel hungry after eating healthy keto diet food.

- Longevity

Keto diet is responsible to increase your lifespan. The keto diet allows you to consume healthy notorious and antioxidant-rich foods. This will help to cures various health-related problems that occur due to the consumption of unhealthy and poor diet. The scientific studies prove that the peoples who follow the keto diet can result in a significant drop in oxidative stress level. It also reduces the risk of diabetes, heart disease, and obesity and improves lifespan.

- Increase in energy levels

The keto diet shifts your body to breakdown fats for energy instead of glucose. During the fat breaking, process chemicals are released, and our liver converts it into ketones. Ketones provide energy to our body organ and tissues and long-lasting energy source to our body. Due to an increase in energy level, you feel active and fully energized the whole day.

Tips and Tricks for Successful Keto Journey

The following tips and tricks are helpful to complete your keto journey.

1. Limit Daily Carb Consumption

To stay in ketosis, it is recommended to consume 10 to 30 grams of carb daily. If you are an active person and doing hard exercise for 5 to 6 days a week then you can increase carb consumption. Don't eat too much carb it may build up glycogen storage.

2. **Eat healthy fats**

During the keto diet, it is recommended to eat healthy fats like avocado oil, olive oil, coconut oil, etc. avoid unhealthy fats like vegetable oil, sunflower oil, canola oil, etc. Healthy fat consumption will help to boost ketone levels in your body and keep your body in a ketosis state.

3. **Get enough sleep**

Due to Inadequate sleep, you feel hunger and it is one of the bad signs for your weight loss process. To stay in ketosis during the keto diet you need not only enough sleep but also get better quality sleep. Better quality means you should sleep in a cool and darkroom. The room temperature is maintained at 65 F and you need to sleep at least 7 hours a daily night to get complete enough sleep.

4. **Consume Moderate Protein**

In the keto diet our body breaks down fats for energy. In this fat breaking process some healthy muscles and fats. An adequate amount of protein consumption will help to repair this muscle and also maintain muscle mass. As per your body weight, it is recommended to consume 0.75 grams of protein per pound.

5. **Regular exercise**

Regular exercise during the keto diet will keep you energized throughout the day. It also increases the ketones level and decreases the carb from your body. Regular exercise keeps you fit and also maintains your blood sugar level.

6. **Use MCT oils**

Use coconut oil which contains healthy fats called MCT (Medium Chain Triglycerides). It is easily absorbed by the liver and converts into ketones. MCT oils provide an instant source of energy to our body and are converted into ketones. MCTs travel fast into your body and enter into your body cells without broken.

7. **Stay Hydrated**

When you follow the keto diet, it is important to keep your body hydrated. During the diet period, your body loses glycogens through the urination process. These glycogens hold 5 parts of water, so your body is dehydrated during the diet. To keep your body hydrated you need to consume smoothies, coffee, or tea during the diet period.

Chapter 2: The Basics of PowerXL Grill Air Fryer Combo

What is PowerXL Grill Air Fryer Combo?

The PowerXL Grill is an advanced and smart cooking device made with a combination of grill and air fryer. The PowerXL grill is one of the 12 in 1 multifunctional device and one of the best-selling indoor grills available in the market. It is capable to perform 12 different cooking tasks like Air Fry, Grill, Simmer, Slow Cook, Sous Vide, Steam, Roast, Fry, Sauté, rice and keep warm. You never need to buy a separate cooking appliance for each single cooking task. Your PowerXL grill is capable to handle all these tasks and saves your time in kitchen top space.

The PowerXL Grill is made up of plastic and stainless steel body and requires 1550 watts power to cook your food faster. The grill comes with accessories like inner pot, glass lid, grill plate, and ladle. The inner pot and grill plate come with non-stick coatings and all these accessories are dishwasher safe. The grill plate having char grill marks and having the capability to heat the grill plate to 500°F temperature. It is capable to hold four burgers, six salmon filets, or half chicken. One of the best parts of the grill is it has a slow cooking function you can choose 180°F to 500°F temperature settings for slow cooking purposes. The grill also has a big digital touch control panel system that comes with 12 preset settings. You can easily navigate and select the desire cooking functions as per your recipe needs.

The PowerXL Grill comes with security features like overheat protection. When the inner temperature control system will fail to control the grill temperature properly then the overheat protection system will be activated and the appliances stop working. When these happen then power off and unplug the appliance from the power socket and let it cool down at room temperature before restating it. The PowerXL grill works on rapid crisp technology in which the hot air has circulated the food to cook food faster and you will get even cooking results every time. Using this technique you can cook your food with 80% or less fat and oils compare with the deep-frying method.

Parts and Accessories

- **PowerXL Grill Main Unit**

The main unit of the PowerXL Grill is made up of plastic and stainless steel combination. It requires 1550 watts of power to work and the heating elements can produce a maximum 500°F temperature.

- **Air fryer lid**

The air fryer lid is used when you are using the air frying function. When you are not using the air frying function then detach the lid and place the tempered glass lid while using other cooking functions.

- **Lid Handle**

The air fryer lid comes with a lid handle for your safety purpose. Always use the lid handle to open or close the lid because the lid is too hot during the cooking process.

- **Control Panel**

The PowerXL Grill has a big digital control touch panel system that comes with 12 preset functions and touches control buttons. You can easily navigate between these 12 preset functions by turning the dial button to select desire cooking functions. You can set the cooking time and temperature settings manually by rotating the control dial as per your recipe needs.

- **Inner Pot**

The inner pot of the PowerXL grill comes with no-stick coatings. You can place the other additional accessories into the inner pot. The inner pot is dishwasher safe so you can easily clean it into the dishwasher.

- **Glass lid**

When you are not using air frying functions then you can use a glass lid. Use glass lid while using cooking functions like Slow cook, Steam, Sauté, Rice, Simmer, Sous vide, fry, and keep warm function.

- **Grill Plate**

The non-stick grill plate is used while using air frying functions to circulate hot air under the food. You can also use a grill plate while steaming to keep your food above the liquid present in the pot. While grilling your favorite meats and vegetable you can preheat the grill plate before placing your food on it.

Operating Buttons and Preset Functions

The PowerXL Grill comes with a big digital control panel system and 12 preset functions. Choose an appropriate function from the given preset function as per your recipe needs. More information about these buttons and functions are given as follows:

Preset Functions

1. **Air Fry:** This function is ideal for air frying your favourite food like French fries, chicken wings, vegetables, mozzarella sticks, and more within very little fats and oils. It saves more than 70% of oil and fats compared to the deep frying method without compromising the taste and texture like deep-fried food. While using this function always use air fryer lid.
2. **Slow Cook:** Using this function you can convert your powerXL grill in to slow cooker. It cooks your food at a very low temperature for a long time and brings out flavors into your food. While using this function you can cook a variety of food at a low temperature without losing its nutritional values. Use a glass lid while using this function.
3. **Steam:** This function converts your PowerXL grill into a steamer. A small amount of water reaches its boiling point will create the steam. While using this function use a steaming rack and glass lid.
4. **Sauté:** This function is used as a frying pan. It converts your PowerXL grill into a frying pan for searing your food. While using this function use the glass lid.
5. **Grill:** Using this function you can grill your favorite food. While using this function uses a grill plate for best results. It produces the high heat at 500°F to heat the grill plate. You will get nice grill marks on your food without filling your kitchen with smoke. Use an air fryer lid while using this function.
6. **Bake:** This function is used for baking your favorite cake, cookies, desserts, and more. Use an air fryer lid while using this function.
7. **Roast:** This function is an ideal choice for roasting your favorite food. You can roast the whole piece of fish, vegetables, meat, and more. PowerXL grill uses hot air circulation techniques to roast your food evenly from all sides. While roasting your food you never need to flip your food. Use an air fryer lid while using this function.
8. **Rice:** While using this function the display of the PowerXL grill shows the rotating symbol. The timer will not show the countdown process while using this function because the time will vary and depends upon the quantity of rice

taken. After finishing the cooking cycle the appliances activate keep warm mode. Use a glass lid while using this function.
9. **Simmer:** This function is ideal for simmering your favorite protein (meat, fish, or poultry) at low-temperature settings below boiling points.
10. **Sous Vide:** Using this function you can cook your food like fish and meat by vacuum sealing under a hot water bath. Use a glass lid while using this function.
11. **Fry:** This function is ideal for frying your food (not use for deep frying). It is recommended that do not use more than one inch of oil and set the timer as per recipe needs. Use a glass lid while using this function.
12. **Keep Warm:** This function is used to cook your food slowly for a long period. This function will help to keep your food warm until you serve it. Use a glass lid while using this function.

Operating function

- **Timer Button:** While using some of the cooking modes you can adjust the time settings as per your recipe needs. You just need to press the timer button and adjust the timer settings by turning the control knob. You can also change the time settings at any time during the cooking cycle.
- **Temp Button:** While using some of the cooking modes you can adjust the temperature settings as per your recipe needs. You just need to press the temp button and adjust the desire temperature settings by turning the control knob. You can change the temperature settings at any time during the cooking cycle.
- **Delay Timer:** You can use this function to delay start your cooking process as per your schedule. It allows starting the desire cooking program as per set by your delay time settings.
- **Start Button:** This button is used to start the desire cooking process.
- **Cancel Button:** Using this button you can cancel or stop the current working cooking cycle.
- **Keep Warm:** This function is used to keep your food warm until you served it. To use this function select the desire time settings by turning the control knob. It keeps your food warm for a long time by maintaining a certain temperature.

Cleaning and Maintenance

Regular cleaning is one of the necessary processes done by each use of appliances. It keeps your appliance neat and clean and also increases the lifespan of the appliances. The following simple cleaning steps will help you to clean your PowerXL grill with ease.

1. Before starting the actual cleaning process make sure the appliance is unplugged from the power socket and let it cool down at room temperature.
2. Open the air fryer lid and remove the accessories like the grill plate, and inner pot for cleaning. The accessories come with a PowerXL grill that is dishwasher safe you can clean it using a dishwasher or clean it with soapy water.
3. Do not use harsh chemicals to clean the accessories it may cause to remove the non-stick coating.
4. After cleaning accessories if any residue or stain remains then soak the pot in soapy water for overnight and then clean it properly.
5. Use a clean soft damp cloth to clean the main unit from inside and outside.
6. After finishing the cleaning process make sure all the accessories are dry thoroughly before fixing its original position.
7. Now your PowerXL grill is ready for next use.

Chapter 3: Breakfast

Almond Butter Oatmeal

Preparation Time: 10 minutes
Cooking Time: 35 minutes
Serve: 4

Ingredients:

- 2 cups old fashioned oats
- 1/4 cup maple syrup
- 1/2 cup almond butter
- 2 tsp vanilla
- 1 3/4 cup milk
- 1/4 tsp salt

Directions:

1. In a large bowl, whisk together milk, vanilla, maple syrup, almond butter, and salt. Add oats and stir to mix.
2. Place the inner pot in the PowerXL grill air fryer combo base.
3. Pour oats mixture into the inner pot.
4. Cover the inner pot with air frying lid.
5. Select bake mode then set the temperature to 375 F and time for 35 minutes. Press start.
6. When the timer reaches 0, then press the cancel button.
7. Serve and enjoy.

Nutritional Value (Amount per Serving):

- Calories 435
- Fat 8.5 g
- Carbohydrates 72.8 g
- Sugar 19 g
- Protein 13.9 g
- Cholesterol 9 mg

Healthy Spinach Frittata

Preparation Time: 10 minutes
Cooking Time: 10 minutes
Serve: 6

Ingredients:

- 6 large eggs
- 1 cup fresh spinach, chopped
- 1/2 cup cheddar cheese, shredded
- 1/4 tsp onion powder
- 1/4 tsp garlic powder
- 1/8 tsp black pepper
- 1/4 tsp salt

Directions:

1. In a bowl, whisk together eggs with onion powder, garlic powder, pepper, and salt.
2. Add spinach and cheese and stir well.
3. Place the inner pot in the PowerXL grill air fryer combo base.
4. Pour egg mixture into the inner pot.
5. Cover the inner pot with air frying lid.
6. Select bake mode then set the temperature to 400 F and time for 10 minutes. Press start.
7. When the timer reaches 0, then press the cancel button.
8. Slice and serve.

Nutritional Value (Amount per Serving):

- Calories 135
- Fat 10.4 g
- Carbohydrates 1 g
- Sugar 0.4 g
- Protein 9 g
- Cholesterol 196 mg

Delicious Jalapeno Bread

Preparation Time: 10 minutes
Cooking Time: 15 minutes
Serve: 4

Ingredients:

- 4 large eggs
- 1/4 cup parmesan cheese, grated
- 1/2 tsp pepper
- 1/2 tsp garlic powder
- 4 jalapeno chilies, chopped
- 1/4 tsp baking powder
- 1/3 cup coconut flour
- 1/2 cup cheddar cheese, grated
- 1/4 cup water
- 1/4 cup butter
- 1/2 tsp salt

Directions:

1. In a bowl, combine together eggs, pepper, salt, water, and butter.
2. Add baking powder, garlic powder, and coconut flour and mix until well combined.
3. Add jalapenos, cheddar cheese, and parmesan cheese. Mix well.
4. Place the inner pot in the PowerXL grill air fryer combo base.
5. Pour batter into the inner pot and spread evenly.
6. Cover the inner pot with air frying lid.
7. Select bake mode then set the temperature to 400 F and time for 15 minutes. Press start.
8. When the timer reaches 0, then press the cancel button.
9. Slice and serve.

Nutritional Value (Amount per Serving):

- Calories 250
- Fat 22 g
- Carbohydrates 2.7 g
- Sugar 1.1 g
- Protein 11.1 g
- Cholesterol 233 mg

Healthy Spinach Frittata

Preparation Time: 10 minutes
Cooking Time: 20 minutes
Serve: 2

Ingredients:

- 6 eggs
- 2 oz butter
- 5 oz mushrooms, sliced
- 4 oz feta cheese, crumbled
- 2 oz green onions, chopped
- 3 oz fresh spinach, chopped
- Pepper
- Salt

Directions:

1. Place the inner pot in the PowerXL grill air fryer combo base.
2. Select sauté mode and press start.
3. Add butter into the inner pot.
4. Once butter is melted then add mushrooms and green onions and sauté for 5-10 minutes.
5. Add spinach and sauté for 2 minutes.
6. Press the cancel button.
7. In a bowl, whisk eggs, cheese, pepper, and salt.
8. Pour egg mixture over the mushroom mixture.
9. Cover the inner pot with air frying lid.
10. Select bake mode then set the temperature to 350 F and time for 20 minutes. Press start.
11. When the timer reaches 0, then press the cancel button.
12. Serve and enjoy.

Nutritional Value (Amount per Serving):

- Calories 576
- Fat 48.6 g
- Carbohydrates 9.3 g
- Sugar 5.4 g
- Protein 28.9 g
- Cholesterol 602 mg

Delicious Berry Oatmeal

Preparation Time: 10 minutes
Cooking Time: 20 minutes
Serve: 4

Ingredients:

- 1 egg
- 1/4 cup maple syrup
- 1 1/2 cups milk
- 1 cup blueberries
- 1/2 cup blackberries
- 1 1/2 tsp baking powder
- 2 cups old fashioned oats
- 1/2 cup strawberries
- 1/2 tsp salt

Directions:

1. In a mixing bowl, mix together oats, salt, and baking powder.
2. Add vanilla, egg, maple syrup, and milk and stir well. Add berries and stir well.
3. Place the inner pot in the PowerXL grill air fryer combo base.
4. Pour mixture into the inner pot.
5. Cover the inner pot with air frying lid.
6. Select bake mode then set the temperature to 375 F and time for 20 minutes. Press start.
7. When the timer reaches 0, then press the cancel button.
8. Serve and enjoy.

Nutritional Value (Amount per Serving):

- Calories 461
- Fat 8.4 g
- Carbohydrates 80.7 g
- Sugar 23.4 g
- Protein 15 g
- Cholesterol 48 mg

Nutritious Zucchini Muffins

Preparation Time: 10 minutes
Cooking Time: 30 minutes
Serve: 8

Ingredients:

- 1 zucchini, grated
- 3/4 cup applesauce
- 1 tsp liquid stevia
- 1/2 tsp baking soda
- 1 cup almond flour
- 1/4 cup olive oil
- 1/2 cup walnut, chopped
- 1 1/2 tsp cinnamon
- 1/2 cup coconut flour
- 1/8 tsp salt

Directions:

1. In a bowl, mix grated zucchini, coconut oil, and stevia.
2. In a separate bowl, mix together coconut flour, baking soda, almond flour, walnut, cinnamon, and salt.
3. Add zucchini mixture into the coconut flour mixture and mix well.
4. Add applesauce and stir until well combined.
5. Pour batter into the 8 silicone muffin molds.
6. Place the inner pot in the PowerXL grill air fryer combo base.
7. Place muffin molds into the inner pot.
8. Cover the inner pot with air frying lid.
9. Select bake mode then set the temperature to 325 F and time for 30 minutes. Press start.
10. When the timer reaches 0, then press the cancel button.
11. Serve and enjoy.

Nutritional Value (Amount per Serving):

- Calories 230
- Fat 18.9 g
- Carbohydrates 12.5 g
- Sugar 3.4 g
- Protein 5.2 g
- Cholesterol 0 mg

Artichoke Mushroom Quiche

Preparation Time: 10 minutes
Cooking Time: 40 minutes
Serve: 4

Ingredients:

- 3 eggs
- 1 cup artichoke hearts, chopped
- 1 cup mushrooms, sliced
- 10 oz spinach, frozen
- 1 small onion, chopped
- 1/2 tsp olive oil
- 1 tbsp garlic, minced
- 1/2 cup cottage cheese
- Pepper
- Salt

Directions:

1. Place the inner pot in the PowerXL grill air fryer combo base.
2. Select sauté mode and press start.
3. Add olive oil into the inner pot and heat the oil.
4. Add onion, mushrooms, garlic, and spinach and sauté until onion is softened.
5. Press the cancel button.
6. Add cheese and artichoke hearts into the inner pot and mix well.
7. In a bowl, whisk eggs, pepper, and salt and pour into the inner pot.
8. Cover the inner pot with air frying lid.
9. Select bake mode then set the temperature to 350 F and time for 40 minutes. Press start.
10. When the timer reaches 0, then press the cancel button.
11. Serve and enjoy.

Nutritional Value (Amount per Serving):

- Calories 108
- Fat 4.8 g
- Carbohydrates 6.8 g
- Sugar 1.7 g
- Protein 10.9 g
- Cholesterol 125 mg

Blueberry Oatmeal

Preparation Time: 10 minutes
Cooking Time: 40 minutes
Serve: 6

Ingredients:

- 2 cups old-fashioned oats
- 1/4 cup maple syrup
- 2 cups milk
- 1 tsp baking powder
- 1/2 cup pecans, chopped
- 1 tsp ground cinnamon
- 2 cups blueberries
- 2 tsp vanilla
- 1 tbsp coconut oil, melted
- 2 tbsp flaxseed
- 1/2 tsp salt

Directions:

1. Place the inner pot in the PowerXL grill air fryer combo base.
2. Add 1 cup of blueberries into the inner pot.
3. In a large bowl, mix together oats, baking powder, cinnamon, pecans, and salt and sprinkle over blueberries.
4. In a small bowl, mix together milk, vanilla, oil, flaxseed, and maple syrup and pour over the oat mixture. Gently press down the oat mixture.
5. Sprinkle remaining blueberries on top of the oat mixture.
6. Cover the inner pot with air frying lid.
7. Select bake mode then set the temperature to 375 F and time for 40 minutes. Press start.
8. When the timer reaches 0, then press the cancel button.
9. Serve and enjoy.

Nutritional Value (Amount per Serving):

- Calories 380
- Fat 21.3 g
- Carbohydrates 42 g
- Sugar 17.4 g
- Protein 9 g
- Cholesterol 7 mg

Healthy Kale Zucchini Bake

Preparation Time: 10 minutes
Cooking Time: 35 minutes
Serve: 4

Ingredients:

- 6 eggs
- 1 cup cheddar cheese, shredded
- 1 cup kale, chopped
- 1 onion, chopped
- 1 cup zucchini, shredded & squeezed
- 1/2 tsp dill
- 1/2 tsp oregano
- 1/2 tsp basil
- 1/2 tsp baking powder
- 1/2 cup almond flour
- 1/2 cup milk
- Pepper
- Salt

Directions:

1. In a large bowl, whisk eggs with milk.
2. Add remaining ingredients and stir until well combined.
3. Place the inner pot in the PowerXL grill air fryer combo base.
4. Pour egg mixture into the inner pot.
5. Cover the inner pot with air frying lid.
6. Select bake mode then set the temperature to 375 F and time for 35 minutes. Press start.
7. When the timer reaches 0, then press the cancel button.
8. Serve and enjoy.

Nutritional Value (Amount per Serving):

- Calories 329
- Fat 23.7 g
- Carbohydrates 11.2 g
- Sugar 4.2 g
- Protein 20.5 g
- Cholesterol 278 mg

Healthy Oat Breakfast Muffins

Preparation Time: 10 minutes
Cooking Time: 30 minutes
Serve: 12

Ingredients:

- 2 cups oat flour
- 1 tsp vanilla
- 1/3 cup coconut oil, melted
- 1/2 cup maple syrup
- 1 cup applesauce
- 1 tsp cinnamon
- 2 tsp baking powder
- 1/4 tsp salt

Directions:

1. In a bowl, add applesauce, cinnamon, vanilla, oil, maple syrup, and salt and stir to combine.
2. Add baking powder and oat flour and stir well. Let the batter sit for 10 minutes.
3. Spoon batter into the silicone muffin molds.
4. Place the inner pot in the PowerXL grill air fryer combo base.
5. Place muffin molds into the inner pot.
6. Cover the inner pot with air frying lid.
7. Select bake mode then set the temperature to 350 F and time for 30 minutes. Press start.
8. When the timer reaches 0, then press the cancel button.
9. Serve and enjoy.

Nutritional Value (Amount per Serving):

- Calories 158
- Fat 7.1 g
- Carbohydrates 22.2 g
- Sugar 9.9 g
- Protein 2 g
- Cholesterol 0 mg

Chapter 4: Poultry

Chicken Shawarma

Preparation Time: 10 minutes
Cooking Time: 3 hours
Serve: 5

Ingredients:

- 1 1/4 lbs chicken thigh, skinless and boneless
- 1 tsp garlic powder
- 1 tsp cumin
- 2 tbsp garlic, minced
- 1/2 cup Greek yogurt
- 1/4 cup chicken stock
- 1/4 tsp ground coriander
- 1/4 tsp cinnamon
- 1/2 tsp curry powder
- 1/2 tsp dried parsley
- 1 tsp paprika
- 1/4 cup fresh lemon juice
- 1 1/2 tbsp tahini
- 1 tbsp olive oil
- Pepper
- Salt

Directions:

1. Place the inner pot in the PowerXL grill air fryer combo base.
2. Add all ingredients into the inner pot and mix well.
3. Cover the inner pot with a glass lid.
4. Select slow cook mode then press the temperature button and set the time for 3 hours. Press start.
5. When the timer reaches 0, then press the cancel button.
6. Serve and enjoy.

Nutritional Value (Amount per Serving):

- Calories 295
- Fat 14.3 g
- Carbohydrates 4.2 g
- Sugar 1.4 g
- Protein 36.2 g
- Cholesterol 102 mg

Roasted Pepper Chicken

Preparation Time: 10 minutes
Cooking Time: 4 hours
Serve: 4

Ingredients:

- 2 lbs chicken breasts, skinless and boneless
- 3 tbsp red wine vinegar
- 1 onion, diced
- 1/2 cup olives
- 10 oz roasted red peppers, drained and chopped
- 1/2 cup feta cheese, crumbled
- 1 tsp dried thyme
- 1 tsp dried oregano
- 1 tbsp garlic, minced
- 1 tbsp olive oil
- 1/4 tsp pepper
- 1/2 tsp kosher salt

Directions:

1. Place the inner pot in the PowerXL grill air fryer combo base.
2. Add all ingredients into the inner pot and mix well.
3. Cover the inner pot with a glass lid.
4. Select slow cook mode then press the temperature button and set the time for 4 hours. Press start.
5. When the timer reaches 0, then press the cancel button.
6. Serve and enjoy.

Nutritional Value (Amount per Serving):

- Calories 567
- Fat 26.3 g
- Carbohydrates 10 g
- Sugar 5.1 g
- Protein 69.6 g
- Cholesterol 219 mg

Chicken Paillard

Preparation Time: 10 minutes
Cooking Time: 25 minutes
Serve: 8

Ingredients:

- 4 chicken breasts, skinless and boneless
- 1/2 cup olives, diced
- 1 small onion, sliced
- 1 fennel bulb, sliced
- 28 oz can tomatoes, diced
- 1/4 cup fresh basil, chopped
- 1/4 cup fresh parsley, chopped
- 1/4 cup pine nuts
- 2 tbsp olive oil
- Pepper
- Salt

Directions:

1. Arrange chicken in baking dish and season with pepper and salt and drizzle with oil.
2. In a bowl, mix together olives, tomatoes, pine nuts, onion, fennel, pepper, and salt.
3. Pour olive mixture over chicken.
4. Place the inner pot in the PowerXL grill air fryer combo base.
5. Place baking dish into the inner pot.
6. Cover the inner pot with an air frying lid.
7. Select bake mode then set the temperature to 450 F and time for 25 minutes. Press start.
8. When the timer reaches 0, then press the cancel button.
9. Serve and enjoy.

Nutritional Value (Amount per Serving):

- Calories 242
- Fat 12.8 g
- Carbohydrates 9.3 g
- Sugar 3.9 g
- Protein 23.2 g
- Cholesterol 65 mg

Chicken Fajita Casserole

Preparation Time: 10 minutes
Cooking Time: 15 minutes
Serve: 4

Ingredients:

- 1 lb cooked chicken, shredded
- 7 oz cheddar cheese, shredded
- 2 tbsp tex-mix seasoning
- 1 onion, sliced
- 1 bell pepper, sliced
- 1/3 cup mayonnaise
- 7 oz cream cheese
- Pepper
- Salt

Directions:

1. Mix all ingredients except 2 oz shredded cheese in a baking dish.
2. Spread remaining cheese on top.
3. Place the inner pot in the PowerXL grill air fryer combo base.
4. Place baking dish into the inner pot.
5. Cover the inner pot with an air frying lid.
6. Select bake mode then set the temperature to 390 F and time for 15 minutes. Press start.
7. When the timer reaches 0, then press the cancel button.
8. Serve and enjoy.

Nutritional Value (Amount per Serving):

- Calories 641
- Fat 44.1 g
- Carbohydrates 13.3 g
- Sugar 4.3 g
- Protein 50.2 g
- Cholesterol 199 mg

Greek Tomato Olive Chicken

Preparation Time: 10 minutes
Cooking Time: 18 minutes
Serve: 4

Ingredients:

- 4 chicken breast, boneless and halves
- 15 olives, pitted and halved
- 2 cups cherry tomatoes
- 3 tbsp olive oil
- 3 tbsp capers, rinsed and drained
- Pepper
- Salt

Directions:

1. In a bowl, toss tomatoes, capers, olives, and olive oil. Set aside.
2. Season chicken with pepper and salt.
3. Place chicken in the baking dish and top with tomato mixture.
4. Place the inner pot in the PowerXL grill air fryer combo base.
5. Place baking dish into the inner pot.
6. Cover the inner pot with an air frying lid.
7. Select bake mode then set the temperature to 475 F and time for 18 minutes. Press start.
8. When the timer reaches 0, then press the cancel button.
9. Serve and enjoy.

Nutritional Value (Amount per Serving):

- Calories 241
- Fat 15 g
- Carbohydrates 4.9 g
- Sugar 2.4 g
- Protein 22.3 g
- Cholesterol 64 mg

Apple Chicken

Preparation Time: 10 minutes
Cooking Time: 45 minutes
Serve: 2

Ingredients:

- 2 chicken breasts, skinless and boneless
- 12 Ritz cracker, crushed
- 10 oz can condensed cheddar cheese soup
- 1 apple, sliced
- Pepper
- Salt

Directions:

1. Season chicken with pepper and salt and place into the baking dish.
2. Arrange sliced apple on top of chicken. Sprinkle crushed crackers on top.
3. Place the inner pot in the PowerXL grill air fryer combo base.
4. Place baking dish into the inner pot.
5. Cover the inner pot with an air frying lid.
6. Select bake mode then set the temperature to 350 F and time for 45 minutes. Press start.
7. When the timer reaches 0, then press the cancel button.
8. Serve and enjoy.

Nutritional Value (Amount per Serving):

- Calories 924
- Fat 38.2 g
- Carbohydrates 87 g
- Sugar 21.4 g
- Protein 51.8 g
- Cholesterol 136 mg

Honey Mustard Chicken

Preparation Time: 10 minutes
Cooking Time: 4 hours
Serve: 2

Ingredients:

- 1 lb chicken breast, skinless, boneless and cut into pieces
- 2 tbsp soy sauce
- 1/4 cup orange juice
- 1/2 cup ground mustard
- 1/4 cup honey
- 2 tbsp water
- 2 tbsp cornstarch

Directions:

1. Place the inner pot in the PowerXL grill air fryer combo base.
2. Add chicken into the inner pot.
3. In a small bowl, combine together soy sauce, orange juice, ground mustard, and honey.
4. Pour bowl mixture over the chicken.
5. Cover the inner pot with a glass lid.
6. Select slow cook mode then press the temperature button and set the time for 4 hours. Press start.
7. When the timer reaches 0, then press the cancel button.
8. Mix together water and cornstarch and pour over the chicken mixture and stir well.
9. Serve and enjoy.

Nutritional Value (Amount per Serving):

- Calories 626
- Fat 17.1 g
- Carbohydrates 60.5 g
- Sugar 40.4 g
- Protein 59.3 g
- Cholesterol 145 mg

Simple & Easy Slow Cook Chicken

Preparation Time: 10 minutes
Cooking Time: 4 hours
Serve: 2

Ingredients:

- 1 1/4 lbs chicken, boneless
- 8 oz salsa
- 7 oz condensed cheddar soup

Directions:

1. Place the inner pot in the PowerXL grill air fryer combo base.
2. Add all ingredients into the inner pot and mix well.
3. Cover the inner pot with a glass lid.
4. Select slow cook mode then press the temperature button and set the time for 4 hours. Press start.
5. When the timer reaches 0, then press the cancel button.
6. Shred the chicken using a fork and serve.

Nutritional Value (Amount per Serving):

- Calories 550
- Fat 12.9 g
- Carbohydrates 17 g
- Sugar 5.1 g
- Protein 85.6 g
- Cholesterol 222 mg

Tender & Juicy Chicken

Preparation Time: 10 minutes
Cooking Time: 40 minutes
Serve: 6

Ingredients:

- 2 lbs chicken thighs, skinless and boneless
- 8 garlic cloves, sliced
- 2 tbsp olive oil
- 2 tbsp fresh parsley, chopped
- 1 fresh lemon juice
- Pepper
- Salt

Directions:

1. Place chicken on a baking dish and season with pepper and salt.
2. Sprinkle parsley and garlic over the chicken and drizzle oil and lemon juice on top of the chicken.
3. Place the inner pot in the PowerXL grill air fryer combo base.
4. Place baking dish in the inner pot.
5. Cover the inner pot with an air frying lid.
6. Select bake mode then set the temperature to 450 F and time for 40 minutes. Press start.
7. When the timer reaches 0, then press the cancel button.
8. Serve and enjoy.

Nutritional Value (Amount per Serving):

- Calories 336
- Fat 16 g
- Carbohydrates 1.6 g
- Sugar 0.2 g
- Protein 44.1 g
- Cholesterol 135 mg

Greek Chicken

Preparation Time: 10 minutes
Cooking Time: 6 hours
Serve: 4

Ingredients:

- 4 chicken breasts, skinless and boneless
- 1/4 cup fresh lemon juice
- 2 tsp dried oregano
- 1 tbsp garlic, minced
- 1 cup chicken stock
- 3/4 tbsp lemon zest
- 1 tsp kosher salt

Directions:

1. Place the inner pot in the PowerXL grill air fryer combo base.
2. Add all ingredients into the inner pot and mix well.
3. Cover the inner pot with a glass lid.
4. Select slow cook mode then press the temperature button and set the time for 6 hours. Press start.
5. When the timer reaches 0, then press the cancel button.
6. Serve and enjoy.

Nutritional Value (Amount per Serving):

- Calories 290
- Fat 11.2 g
- Carbohydrates 1.9 g
- Sugar 0.6 g
- Protein 42.8 g
- Cholesterol 130 mg

Tasty Caribbean Chicken

Preparation Time: 10 minutes
Cooking Time: 10 minutes
Serve: 8

Ingredients:

- 3 lbs chicken thigh, skinless and boneless
- 3 tbsp coconut oil, melted
- 1/2 tsp ground nutmeg
- 1/2 tsp ground ginger
- 1 tbsp cayenne
- 1 tbsp cinnamon
- 1 tbsp coriander powder
- Pepper
- Salt

Directions:

1. In a small bowl, mix together all ingredients except chicken.
2. Rub bowl mixture all over the chicken.
3. Place the inner pot in the PowerXL grill air fryer combo base.
4. Place grill plate in the inner pot. Cover.
5. Select air fry mode then set the temperature to 390 F and time for 10 minutes. Press start.
6. Let the appliance preheat for 3 minutes.
7. Open the lid then place chicken on the grill plate.
8. Serve and enjoy.

Nutritional Value (Amount per Serving):

- Calories 373
- Fat 17.9 g
- Carbohydrates 1.2 g
- Sugar 0.1 g
- Protein 49.3 g
- Cholesterol 151 mg

Crispy Crusted Chicken

Preparation Time: 10 minutes
Cooking Time: 30 minutes
Serve: 4

Ingredients:

- 1 egg, lightly beaten
- 2 tbsp butter, melted
- 4 chicken breasts, skinless and boneless
- 1 tsp water
- 3 cups corn flakes, crushed
- 1 tsp poultry seasoning
- Pepper
- Salt

Directions:

1. Season chicken with poultry seasoning, pepper, and salt.
2. In a shallow bowl, whisk together egg and water.
3. In a separate shallow bowl, mix together crushed cornflakes and melted butter.
4. Dip chicken into the egg mixture then coats with crushed cornflakes.
5. Place the inner pot in the PowerXL grill air fryer combo base.
6. Place the coated chicken into the inner pot.
7. Cover the inner pot with an air frying lid.
8. Select bake mode then set the temperature to 400 F and time for 30 minutes. Press start.
9. When the timer reaches 0, then press the cancel button.
10. Serve and enjoy.

Nutritional Value (Amount per Serving):

- Calories 421
- Fat 17.7 g
- Carbohydrates 18.6 g
- Sugar 1.5 g
- Protein 45.1 g
- Cholesterol 186 mg

Chili Garlic Chicken Wings

Preparation Time: 10 minutes
Cooking Time: 20 minutes
Serve: 4

Ingredients:

- 12 chicken wings
- 1 tsp granulated garlic
- 1 tbsp chili powder
- 1/2 tbsp baking powder
- 1/2 tsp sea salt

Directions:

1. Add chicken wings into the large bowl and toss with remaining ingredients.
2. Place the inner pot in the PowerXL grill air fryer combo base.
3. Place grill plate in the inner pot. Cover.
4. Select air fry mode then set the temperature to 410 F and time for 20 minutes. Press start.
5. Let the appliance preheat for 3 minutes.
6. Open the lid then place chicken wings on the grill plate.
7. Serve and enjoy.

Nutritional Value (Amount per Serving):

- Calories 580
- Fat 22.6 g
- Carbohydrates 2.4 g
- Sugar 0.3 g
- Protein 87.1 g
- Cholesterol 267 mg

Mexican Chicken Lasagna

Preparation Time: 10 minutes
Cooking Time: 15 minutes
Serve: 15

Ingredients:

- 1 1/2 lbs chicken breast, cooked and shredded
- 3/4 cup sour cream
- 2 cup cheese, shredded
- 4 tortillas
- 1 tsp dry onion, minced
- 2 tsp ground cumin
- 2 tbsp chili powder
- 1 cup of salsa

Directions:

1. Mix together chicken, dried onion, cumin, chili powder, salsa, and sour cream.
2. Spread half chicken mixture in a baking dish then place 2 tortillas on top.
3. Sprinkle 1/2 cheese over the tortillas then repeat the layers.
4. Place the inner pot in the PowerXL grill air fryer combo base.
5. Place baking dish into the inner pot.
6. Cover the inner pot with an air frying lid.
7. Select bake mode then set the temperature to 390 F and time for 15 minutes. Press start.
8. When the timer reaches 0, then press the cancel button.
9. Serve and enjoy.

Nutritional Value (Amount per Serving):

- Calories 160
- Fat 9 g
- Carbohydrates 5.3 g
- Sugar 0.8 g
- Protein 14.5 g
- Cholesterol 50 mg

Delicious Tandoori Chicken

Preparation Time: 10 minutes
Cooking Time: 15 minutes
Serve: 4

Ingredients:

- 1 lb chicken tenders, cut in half
- 1/4 cup yogurt
- 1 tsp paprika
- 1 tsp garam masala
- 1 tsp turmeric
- 1 tsp cayenne pepper
- 1/4 cup parsley, chopped
- 1 tbsp garlic, minced
- 1 tbsp ginger, minced
- 1 tsp salt

Directions:

1. Add all ingredients into the large bowl and mix well. Place in refrigerator for 30 minutes.
2. Place the inner pot in the PowerXL grill air fryer combo base.
3. Place grill plate in the inner pot. Cover.
4. Select air fry mode then set the temperature to 350 F and time for 15 minutes. Press start.
5. Let the appliance preheat for 3 minutes.
6. Open the lid then place marinated chicken on the grill plate.
7. Serve and enjoy.

Nutritional Value (Amount per Serving):

- Calories 240
- Fat 8.9 g
- Carbohydrates 3.9 g
- Sugar 1.3 g
- Protein 34.2 g
- Cholesterol 102 mg

Easy Slow Cook Chicken

Preparation Time: 10 minutes
Cooking Time: 4 hours
Serve: 4

Ingredients:

- 4 chicken breasts, skinless & boneless
- 1 tsp ground black pepper
- 1 tbsp dried onion, minced
- 10.5 oz can cream of mushroom soup

Directions:

1. Place the inner pot in the PowerXL grill air fryer combo base.
2. Place chicken breasts into the inner pot.
3. Mix together the cream of mushroom soup, onion, and black pepper and pour over the chicken.
4. Cover the inner pot with a glass lid.
5. Select slow cook mode then press the temperature button and set the time for 6 hours. Press start.
6. When the timer reaches 0, then press the cancel button.
7. Serve and enjoy.

Nutritional Value (Amount per Serving):

- Calories 318
- Fat 12.1 g
- Carbohydrates 6.6 g
- Sugar 1.7 g
- Protein 43.2 g
- Cholesterol 132 mg

Spicy Chicken Ginger Soup

Preparation Time: 10 minutes
Cooking Time: 3 hours
Serve: 4

Ingredients:

- 1 lb chicken, cooked and diced
- 14 oz can coconut milk
- 1 tbsp garlic powder
- 1 cup rice, uncooked
- 2 tbsp fresh basil, chopped
- 1 tbsp ground ginger
- 1 tbsp green curry paste
- 2 tsp thyme
- 4 cup chicken stock

Directions:

1. Place the inner pot in the PowerXL grill air fryer combo base.
2. Add all ingredients into the inner pot and mix well.
3. Cover the inner pot with a glass lid.
4. Select slow cook mode then press the temperature button and set the time for 3 hours. Press start.
5. When the timer reaches 0, then press the cancel button.
6. Serve and enjoy.

Nutritional Value (Amount per Serving):

- Calories 599
- Fat 28.8 g
- Carbohydrates 46.4 g
- Sugar 4.6 g
- Protein 39.6 g
- Cholesterol 87 mg

Broccoli Chicken Casserole

Preparation Time: 10 minutes
Cooking Time: 45 minutes
Serve: 4

Ingredients:

- 4 chicken breasts, skinless & boneless
- 1 cup Ritz crackers, crushed
- 1/2 tsp paprika
- 10.5 oz can cheddar cheese soup
- 10 oz frozen broccoli florets
- 1 cup sharp cheddar cheese, shredded
- 1 cup milk
- Black pepper
- Kosher salt

Directions:

1. Place the inner pot in the PowerXL grill air fryer combo base.
2. Season chicken with pepper and salt and place into the inner pot.
3. In a large bowl, mix together milk, cheddar cheese, paprika, cheddar cheese soup, half crackers, and broccoli and pour over chicken.
4. Top with remaining crackers.
5. Cover the inner pot with an air frying lid.
6. Select bake mode then set the temperature to 350 F and time for 45 minutes. Press start.
7. When the timer reaches 0, then press the cancel button.
8. Serve and enjoy.

Nutritional Value (Amount per Serving):

- Calories 533
- Fat 25.4 g
- Carbohydrates 16.5 g
- Sugar 6.1 g
- Protein 53.6 g
- Cholesterol 168 mg

Baked Chicken Mushrooms

Preparation Time: 10 minutes
Cooking Time: 30 minutes
Serve: 4

Ingredients:

- 2 lbs chicken breasts, halved
- 1/3 cup sun-dried tomatoes
- 8 oz mushrooms, sliced
- 1/2 cup mayonnaise
- 1 tsp salt

Directions:

1. Grease baking dish with butter and set aside.
2. Place chicken into the baking dish and top with sun-dried tomatoes, mushrooms, mayonnaise, and salt. Mix well.
3. Place the inner pot in the PowerXL grill air fryer combo base.
4. Place baking dish into the inner pot.
5. Cover the inner pot with an air frying lid.
6. Select bake mode then set the temperature to 390 F and time for 30 minutes. Press start.
7. When the timer reaches 0, then press the cancel button.
8. Serve and enjoy.

Nutritional Value (Amount per Serving):

- Calories 560
- Fat 26.8 g
- Carbohydrates 9.5 g
- Sugar 3.2 g
- Protein 67.8 g
- Cholesterol 209 mg

Meatballs

Preparation Time: 10 minutes
Cooking Time: 10 minutes
Serve: 4

Ingredients:

- 1 lb ground chicken
- 1 tbsp soy sauce
- 1/4 cup shredded coconut
- 1 tsp sesame oil
- 1 tsp sriracha
- 1 tbsp hoisin sauce
- 1/2 cup fresh cilantro, chopped
- 2 green onions, chopped
- Pepper
- Salt

Directions:

1. Add all ingredients into the large bowl and mix until well combined.
2. Make small balls from the meat mixture.
3. Place the inner pot in the PowerXL grill air fryer combo base.
4. Place grill plate in the inner pot. Cover.
5. Select air fry mode then set the temperature to 350 F and time for 10 minutes. Press start.
6. Let the appliance preheat for 3 minutes.
7. Open the lid then place meatballs on the grill plate.
8. Serve and enjoy.

Nutritional Value (Amount per Serving):

- Calories 258
- Fat 11.4 g
- Carbohydrates 3.7 g
- Sugar 1.7 g
- Protein 33.5 g
- Cholesterol 101 mg

Chicken with Artichoke Hearts

Preparation Time: 10 minutes
Cooking Time: 8 hours
Serve: 6

Ingredients:

- 6 chicken thighs, skinless and boneless
- 3 tbsp fresh lemon juice
- 10 oz frozen artichoke hearts
- 14 oz can tomatoes, diced
- 1/2 tsp garlic powder
- 1 tsp dried basil
- 1 tsp dried oregano
- 15 olives, pitted
- Pepper
- Salt

Directions:

1. Place the inner pot in the PowerXL grill air fryer combo base.
2. Add all ingredients into the inner pot and mix well.
3. Cover the inner pot with a glass lid.
4. Select slow cook mode then press the temperature button and set the time for 8 hours. Press start.
5. When the timer reaches 0, then press the cancel button.
6. Serve and enjoy.

Nutritional Value (Amount per Serving):

- Calories 330
- Fat 12.2 g
- Carbohydrates 9.5 g
- Sugar 3 g
- Protein 44.6 g
- Cholesterol 130 mg

Chicken Cacciatore

Preparation Time: 10 minutes
Cooking Time: 5 hours
Serve: 2

Ingredients:

- 1 3/4 lb chicken thighs
- 1 cherry pepper
- 1 small onion, chopped
- 6 oz cremini mushrooms
- 1 medium red pepper
- 14 oz tomato paste
- 1 tbsp capers
- 1 fresh rosemary sprig
- 1 garlic clove
- 1 cup chicken broth
- Pepper
- Salt

Directions:

1. Place the inner pot in the PowerXL grill air fryer combo base.
2. Whisk together tomato paste and broth in a bowl.
3. Season chicken with pepper and salt.
4. Place season chicken into the inner pot.
5. Add remaining ingredients to the inner pot then pour tomato paste mixture over chicken.
6. Cover the inner pot with a glass lid.
7. Select slow cook mode then press the temperature button and set the time for 5 hours. Press start.
8. When the timer reaches 0, then press the cancel button.
9. Serve and enjoy.

Nutritional Value (Amount per Serving):

- Calories 1002
- Fat 31.4 g
- Carbohydrates 51.4 g
- Sugar 30.5 g
- Protein 129.2 g
- Cholesterol 353 mg

Asian Chicken Wings

Preparation Time: 10 minutes
Cooking Time: 30 minutes
Serve: 2

Ingredients:

- 4 chicken wings
- 1 tbsp Chinese spice
- 1 tsp mixed spice
- 1 tbsp soy sauce
- Pepper
- Salt

Directions:

1. Add chicken wings into the bowl. Add remaining ingredients and toss well.
2. Place the inner pot in the PowerXL grill air fryer combo base.
3. Place grill plate in the inner pot. Cover.
4. Select air fry mode then set the temperature to 350 F and time for 30 minutes. Press start.
5. Let the appliance preheat for 3 minutes.
6. Open the lid then place chicken wings on the grill plate.
7. Serve and enjoy.

Nutritional Value (Amount per Serving):

- Calories 429
- Fat 17.3 g
- Carbohydrates 2.1 g
- Sugar 0.6 g
- Protein 62.4 g
- Cholesterol 178 mg

Ranch Chicken

Preparation Time: 10 minutes
Cooking Time: 4 hours
Serve: 2

Ingredients:

- 3 chicken breasts, skinless and boneless
- 1 1/2 tbsp dry ranch seasoning
- 1 1/2 tbsp taco seasoning
- 1/4 cup water
- 2 garlic cloves, minced

Directions:

1. Place the inner pot in the PowerXL grill air fryer combo base.
2. Add chicken to the inner pot.
3. In a small bowl, whisk together the remaining ingredients and pour over the chicken.
4. Cover the inner pot with a glass lid.
5. Select slow cook mode then press the temperature button and set the time for 4 hours. Press start.
6. When the timer reaches 0, then press the cancel button.
7. Shred the chicken using a fork and serve.

Nutritional Value (Amount per Serving):

- Calories 465
- Fat 17.5 g
- Carbohydrates 2.6 g
- Sugar 0 g
- Protein 64.8 g
- Cholesterol 198 mg

Caesar Chicken

Preparation Time: 10 minutes
Cooking Time: 6 hours
Serve: 2

Ingredients:

- 2 chicken breasts, skinless and boneless
- 1/4 cup creamy Caesar dressing
- 1/4 tsp dried parsley
- 2 tbsp fresh basil, chopped
- 1/8 tsp black pepper
- 1/8 tsp salt

Directions:

1. Place the inner pot in the PowerXL grill air fryer combo base.
2. Add all ingredients into the inner pot and stir well.
3. Cover the inner pot with a glass lid.
4. Select slow cook mode then press the temperature button and set the time for 6 hours. Press start.
5. When the timer reaches 0, then press the cancel button.
6. Shred the chicken using a fork and serve.

Nutritional Value (Amount per Serving):

- Calories 378
- Fat 19.8 g
- Carbohydrates 3.2 g
- Sugar 2 g
- Protein 42.3 g
- Cholesterol 135 mg

Chapter 5: Beef, Pork & Lamb

Meatballs

Preparation Time: 10 minutes
Cooking Time: 4 hours
Serve: 6

Ingredients:

- 1 egg
- 1/2 lb ground beef
- 1/2 lb ground pork
- 14 oz can tomatoes, crushed
- 2 tbsp fresh basil, chopped
- 2 tbsp fresh parsley, chopped
- 1 garlic clove, minced
- Pepper
- Salt

Directions:

1. Place the inner pot in the PowerXL grill air fryer combo base.
2. In a mixing bowl, mix together beef, pork, egg, parsley, garlic, pepper, and salt until well combined.
3. Make small balls from the meat mixture.
4. Arrange meatballs into the inner pot.
5. Pour crushed tomatoes, basil, pepper, and salt over meatballs.
6. Cover the inner pot with a glass lid.
7. Select slow cook mode then press the temperature button and set the time for 4 hours. Press start.
8. When the timer reaches 0, then press the cancel button.
9. Serve and enjoy.

Nutritional Value (Amount per Serving):

- Calories 150
- Fat 4.4 g
- Carbohydrates 3.7 g
- Sugar 2.3 g
- Protein 23 g
- Cholesterol 89 mg

Italian Beef Roast

Preparation Time: 10 minutes
Cooking Time: 8 hours
Serve: 6

Ingredients:

- 2 lbs lean top round beef roast
- 1 tbsp Italian seasoning
- 6 garlic cloves, minced
- 1 onion, sliced
- 2 cups beef broth
- 1/2 cup red wine
- 1 tsp red pepper flakes
- Pepper
- Salt

Directions:

1. Place the inner pot in the PowerXL grill air fryer combo base.
2. Season meat with pepper and salt and place into the inner pot.
3. Pour remaining ingredients over meat.
4. Cover the inner pot with a glass lid.
5. Select slow cook mode then press the temperature button and set the time for 8 hours. Press start.
6. When the timer reaches 0, then press the cancel button.
7. Remove meat and shred using a fork.
8. Serve and enjoy.

Nutritional Value (Amount per Serving):

- Calories 231
- Fat 6.7 g
- Carbohydrates 4 g
- Sugar 1.4 g
- Protein 35.8 g
- Cholesterol 76 mg

Italian Pork Roast

Preparation Time: 10 minutes
Cooking Time: 6 hours
Serve: 8

Ingredients:

- 2 lbs lean pork roast, boneless
- 1 tbsp parsley
- 1/2 cup parmesan cheese, grated
- 28 oz can tomatoes, diced
- 1 tsp dried oregano
- 1 tsp dried basil
- 1 tsp garlic powder
- Pepper
- Salt

Directions:

1. Place the inner pot in the PowerXL grill air fryer combo base.
2. Add the meat into the inner pot.
3. Mix together tomatoes, oregano, basil, garlic powder, parsley, cheese, pepper, and salt and pour over meat.
4. Cover the inner pot with a glass lid.
5. Select slow cook mode then press the temperature button and set the time for 6 hours. Press start.
6. When the timer reaches 0, then press the cancel button.
7. Serve and enjoy.

Nutritional Value (Amount per Serving):

- Calories 237
- Fat 8.4 g
- Carbohydrates 5.7 g
- Sugar 3.5 g
- Protein 33.7 g
- Cholesterol 94 mg

Shredded Beef

Preparation Time: 10 minutes
Cooking Time: 6 hours
Serve: 2

Ingredients:

- 1 lb beef chuck shoulder roast, boneless and fat trimmed
- 1/2 medium onion, sliced
- 2 banana peppers, sliced
- 1 cup beef broth

Directions:

1. Place the inner pot in the PowerXL grill air fryer combo base.
2. Add all ingredients into the inner pot and mix well.
3. Cover the inner pot with a glass lid.
4. Select slow cook mode then press the temperature button and set the time for 6 hours. Press start.
5. When the timer reaches 0, then press the cancel button.
6. Shred the meat using a fork and serve.

Nutritional Value (Amount per Serving):

- Calories 490
- Fat 27.1 g
- Carbohydrates 12 g
- Sugar 7.5 g
- Protein 46.1 g
- Cholesterol 151 mg

Greek Pork Chops

Preparation Time: 10 minutes
Cooking Time: 6 hours
Serve: 4

Ingredients:

- 4 pork chops, bone-in
- 1 tbsp garlic, minced
- 1/2 small onion, chopped
- 6 oz can tomato paste
- 1/4 tsp red pepper flakes
- 1 tsp Worcestershire sauce
- 1 tbsp dried Italian seasoning
- 1 bell pepper, chopped
- 14.5 oz can tomatoes, diced
- 1/4 tsp pepper
- 1 tsp kosher salt

Directions:

1. Place the inner pot in the PowerXL grill air fryer combo base.
2. Place pork chops into the inner pot.
3. Pour remaining ingredients over the pork chops.
4. Cover the inner pot with a glass lid.
5. Select slow cook mode then press the temperature button and set the time for 6 hours. Press start.
6. When the timer reaches 0, then press the cancel button.
7. Serve and enjoy.

Nutritional Value (Amount per Serving):

- Calories 342
- Fat 21.2 g
- Carbohydrates 17.8 g
- Sugar 11.1 g
- Protein 21.3 g
- Cholesterol 71 mg

Delicious Mongolian Beef

Preparation Time: 10 minutes
Cooking Time: 4 hours
Serve: 2

Ingredients:

- 1 lb sirloin steak, sliced

For sauce:

- 2 tbsp cornstarch
- 1/4 tsp ground ginger
- 1/4 cup water
- 1/4 cup soy sauce
- 1 green onion, sliced
- 1/4 tsp red pepper flakes
- 1/4 cup brown sugar
- 1 tsp garlic, minced

Directions:

1. Place the inner pot in the PowerXL grill air fryer combo base.
2. Add all ingredients into the inner pot and mix well.
3. Cover the inner pot with a glass lid.
4. Select slow cook mode then press the temperature button and set the time for 4 hours. Press start.
5. When the timer reaches 0, then press the cancel button.
6. Serve and enjoy.

Nutritional Value (Amount per Serving):

- Calories 544
- Fat 14.2 g
- Carbohydrates 28.8 g
- Sugar 18.3 g
- Protein 71.1 g
- Cholesterol 203 mg

Beef Fajitas

Preparation Time: 10 minutes
Cooking Time: 8 hours
Serve: 2

Ingredients:

- 1/2 lb beef chuck stew meat
- 1/2 large onion, sliced
- 1 bell pepper, sliced
- 1 tbsp lime juice
- 2 tbsp soy sauce
- 1/2 tsp ground cumin
- 1 tsp chili powder
- 1/4 tsp pepper
- 1/4 tsp salt

Directions:

1. Place the inner pot in the PowerXL grill air fryer combo base.
2. Add all ingredients into the inner pot and mix well.
3. Cover the inner pot with a glass lid.
4. Select slow cook mode then press the temperature button and set the time for 8 hours. Press start.
5. When the timer reaches 0, then press the cancel button.
6. Serve and enjoy.

Nutritional Value (Amount per Serving):

- Calories 191
- Fat 5.6 g
- Carbohydrates 11 g
- Sugar 5.1 g
- Protein 26.3 g
- Cholesterol 70 mg

Salsa Pork Chops

Preparation Time: 10 minutes
Cooking Time: 3 hours
Serve: 8

Ingredients:

- 8 pork chops, bone-in
- 1 tsp garlic powder
- 1/2 tsp ground cumin
- 1/4 cup fresh lime juice
- 1/2 cup salsa
- Pepper
- Salt

Directions:

1. Place the inner pot in the PowerXL grill air fryer combo base.
2. Place pork chops into the inner pot.
3. Pour remaining ingredients over pork chops.
4. Cover the inner pot with a glass lid.
5. Select slow cook mode then press the temperature button and set the time for 3 hours. Press start.
6. When the timer reaches 0, then press the cancel button.
7. Serve and enjoy.

Nutritional Value (Amount per Serving):

- Calories 262
- Fat 19.9 g
- Carbohydrates 1.5 g
- Sugar 0.6 g
- Protein 18.3 g
- Cholesterol 69 mg

Flavorful Steak Fajitas

Preparation Time: 10 minutes
Cooking Time: 4 hours
Serve: 6

Ingredients:

- 2 lbs beef, sliced
- 2 tbsp fajita seasoning
- 20 oz salsa
- 1 onion, sliced
- 2 bell pepper, sliced

Directions:

1. Place the inner pot in the PowerXL grill air fryer combo base.
2. Add salsa into the inner pot.
3. Add meat, bell peppers, onion, and fajita seasoning to the inner pot. Stir well.
4. Cover the inner pot with a glass lid.
5. Select slow cook mode then press the temperature button and set the time for 4 hours. Press start.
6. When the timer reaches 0, then press the cancel button.
7. Serve and enjoy.

Nutritional Value (Amount per Serving):

- Calories 337
- Fat 9.7 g
- Carbohydrates 12.7 g
- Sugar 5.7 g
- Protein 47.9 g
- Cholesterol 135 mg

Delicious Beef Stroganoff

Preparation Time: 10 minutes
Cooking Time: 8 hours
Serve: 2

Ingredients:

- 1/2 lb beef stew meat
- 10 3/4 oz mushroom soup
- 1/4 cup onion, chopped
- 1/2 cup sour cream
- 1/8 tsp pepper
- 2 1/2 oz mushrooms, sliced and drained

Directions:

1. Place the inner pot in the PowerXL grill air fryer combo base.
2. Add all ingredients into the inner pot and mix well.
3. Cover the inner pot with a glass lid.
4. Select slow cook mode then press the temperature button and set the time for 8 hours. Press start.
5. When the timer reaches 0, then press the cancel button.
6. Serve and enjoy.

Nutritional Value (Amount per Serving):

- Calories 477
- Fat 28.2 g
- Carbohydrates 15.3 g
- Sugar 3.5 g
- Protein 40 g
- Cholesterol 127 mg

Beef with Potatoes

Preparation Time: 10 minutes
Cooking Time: 6 hours
Serve: 2

Ingredients:

- 1 lb beef roast
- 3 garlic cloves, minced
- 1 packet onion soup mix
- 16 oz beef broth
- 2 carrots, cut into pieces
- 4 medium potatoes, cleaned and cut into pieces
- 1/2 tsp ground black pepper
- 1/2 tbsp Worcestershire sauce
- 1/2 tbsp adobo seasoning
- Salt

Directions:

1. Place the inner pot in the PowerXL grill air fryer combo base.
2. Add all ingredients into the inner pot and mix well.
3. Cover the inner pot with a glass lid.
4. Select slow cook mode then press the temperature button and set the time for 6 hours. Press start.
5. When the timer reaches 0, then press the cancel button.
6. Serve and enjoy.

Nutritional Value (Amount per Serving):

- Calories 799
- Fat 15.9 g
- Carbohydrates 78.7 g
- Sugar 9.5 g
- Protein 81.7 g
- Cholesterol 203 mg

Beef Ragu

Preparation Time: 10 minutes
Cooking Time: 6 hours
Serve: 2

Ingredients:

- 1 lb chuck roast
- 1/4 cup red wine
- 1/2 tbsp garlic, minced
- 1/2 celery stalk, diced
- 1 small carrot, diced
- 1/4 cup onion, diced
- 1/4 cup water
- 3 oz tomato paste
- 14 oz can tomatoes, crushed
- 1/2 tsp basil
- 1/2 tsp oregano
- 1 beef bouillon
- 1/4 tsp black pepper
- 1/2 tsp salt

Directions:

1. Place the inner pot in the PowerXL grill air fryer combo base.
2. Add all ingredients into the inner pot and mix well.
3. Cover the inner pot with a glass lid.
4. Select slow cook mode then press the temperature button and set the time for 6 hours. Press start.
5. When the timer reaches 0, then press the cancel button.
6. Serve and enjoy.

Nutritional Value (Amount per Serving):

- Calories 623
- Fat 19.5 g
- Carbohydrates 25 g
- Sugar 14.8 g
- Protein 79.8 g
- Cholesterol 229 mg

Moist Pork Roast

Preparation Time: 10 minutes
Cooking Time: 8 hours
Serve: 8

Ingredients:

- 3 lbs pork shoulder
- 1/2 tsp ground sage
- 1/2 tsp ground thyme
- 1 tsp dried basil
- 1/2 cup beef broth
- 1/2 tsp garlic powder
- 1/2 tsp dried rosemary
- 1 tsp dried oregano
- 1/4 tsp pepper
- 1 tsp salt

Directions:

1. Place the inner pot in the PowerXL grill air fryer combo base.
2. Place meat into the inner pot.
3. In a small bowl, mix together garlic powder, rosemary, sage, thyme, basil, oregano, pepper, and salt and sprinkle over meat.
4. Add broth around the meat.
5. Cover the inner pot with a glass lid.
6. Select slow cook mode then press the temperature button and set the time for 8 hours. Press start.
7. When the timer reaches 0, then press the cancel button.
8. Serve and enjoy.

Nutritional Value (Amount per Serving):

- Calories 501
- Fat 36.5 g
- Carbohydrates 0.5 g
- Sugar 0.1 g
- Protein 40 g
- Cholesterol 153 mg

Tender & Moist Lamb Roast

Preparation Time: 10 minutes
Cooking Time: 8 hours
Serve: 8

Ingredients:

- 4 lbs lamb roast, boneless
- 1 tsp oregano
- 1/4 tsp pepper
- 4 garlic cloves, cut into slivers
- 1/2 tsp marjoram
- 1/2 tsp thyme
- 2 tsp salt

Directions:

1. Place the inner pot in the PowerXL grill air fryer combo base.
2. Using a knife make small cuts all over lamb roast then insert garlic slivers into the cuts.
3. In a small bowl, mix marjoram, thyme, oregano, pepper, and salt and rub all over lamb roast.
4. Place lamb roast into the inner pot.
5. Cover the inner pot with a glass lid.
6. Select slow cook mode then press the temperature button and set the time for 8 hours. Press start.
7. When the timer reaches 0, then press the cancel button.
8. Serve and enjoy.

Nutritional Value (Amount per Serving):

- Calories 605
- Fat 48.2 g
- Carbohydrates 0.7 g
- Sugar 0 g
- Protein 38.3 g
- Cholesterol 161 mg

Jalapeno Beef

Preparation Time: 10 minutes
Cooking Time: 6 hours
Serve: 2

Ingredients:

- 1 lb beef chuck roast
- 1/4 cup Worcestershire sauce
- 1/4 cup beef broth
- 6 oz jar roasted bell peppers, drained and chopped
- 2 jalapenos, sliced
- 1/2 onion, sliced
- 1/4 tsp black pepper
- 1/2 tsp salt

Directions:

1. Place the inner pot in the PowerXL grill air fryer combo base.
2. Add all ingredients into the inner pot and mix well.
3. Cover the inner pot with a glass lid.
4. Select slow cook mode then press the temperature button and set the time for 6 hours. Press start.
5. When the timer reaches 0, then press the cancel button.
6. Serve and enjoy.

Nutritional Value (Amount per Serving):

- Calories 874
- Fat 63.4 g
- Carbohydrates 9.7 g
- Sugar 7.7 g
- Protein 60.5 g
- Cholesterol 234 mg

Juicy Pork Tenderloin

Preparation Time: 10 minutes
Cooking Time: 20 minutes
Serve: 4

Ingredients:

- 1 1/2 lbs pork tenderloin
- 1 tsp garlic powder
- 1 tsp Italian seasoning
- 1/4 tsp pepper
- 2 tbsp olive oil
- 1 tsp ground coriander
- 1 tsp sea salt

Directions:

1. Rub pork tenderloin with olive oil.
2. Mix together coriander, garlic powder, Italian seasoning, pepper, and salt and rub over pork tenderloin.
3. Place the inner pot in the PowerXL grill air fryer combo base.
4. Place pork tenderloin in the inner pot.
5. Cover the inner pot with an air frying lid.
6. Select bake mode then set the temperature to 400 F and time for 20 minutes. Press start.
7. When the timer reaches 0, then press the cancel button.
8. Slice and serve.

Nutritional Value (Amount per Serving):

- Calories 310
- Fat 13.3 g
- Carbohydrates 0.7 g
- Sugar 0.3 g
- Protein 44.7 g
- Cholesterol 125 mg

Dijon Pork Chops

Preparation Time: 10 minutes
Cooking Time: 8 hours
Serve: 6

Ingredients:

- 2 lbs pork chops
- 2 tbsp dried oregano
- 2 tbsp Dijon mustard
- 1 tbsp garlic, minced
- 1/4 cup fresh lemon juice
- 3/4 cup olive oil
- 1 tsp dried rosemary
- 1 tsp dried thyme
- 2 tsp dried parsley
- Pepper
- Salt

Directions:

1. Place the inner pot in the PowerXL grill air fryer combo base.
2. Add all ingredients into the inner pot and mix well.
3. Cover the inner pot with a glass lid.
4. Select slow cook mode then press the temperature button and set the time for 8 hours. Press start.
5. When the timer reaches 0, then press the cancel button.
6. Serve and enjoy.

Nutritional Value (Amount per Serving):

- Calories 714
- Fat 63.3 g
- Carbohydrates 2.2 g
- Sugar 0.3 g
- Protein 34.6 g
- Cholesterol 130 mg

Meatballs

Preparation Time: 10 minutes
Cooking Time: 20 minutes
Serve: 4

Ingredients:

- 1 lb ground lamb
- 2 tbsp fresh parsley, chopped
- 1 tbsp garlic, minced
- 1 egg, lightly beaten
- 1/4 tsp pepper
- 1/4 tsp red pepper flakes
- 1 tsp ground cumin
- 2 tsp fresh oregano, chopped
- 1 tsp kosher salt

Directions:

1. Add all ingredients into the mixing bowl and mix until well combined.
2. Make balls from the meat mixture and place them into the inner pot.
3. Place the inner pot in the PowerXL grill air fryer combo base.
4. Place meatballs into the inner pot.
5. Cover the inner pot with an air frying lid.
6. Select bake mode then set the temperature to 425 F and time for 20 minutes. Press start.
7. When the timer reaches 0, then press the cancel button.
8. Serve and enjoy.

Nutritional Value (Amount per Serving):

- Calories 235
- Fat 9.7 g
- Carbohydrates 1.7 g
- Sugar 0.2 g
- Protein 33.6 g
- Cholesterol 143 mg

Pork Chop Cacciatore

Preparation Time: 10 minutes
Cooking Time: 6 hours
Serve: 6

Ingredients:

- 1 1/2 lbs pork chops
- 1 tsp dried oregano
- 3 tbsp tomato paste
- 2 cups mushrooms, sliced
- 1 small onion, diced
- 1 garlic clove, minced
- 1 cup chicken stock
- 14 oz can tomatoes, diced
- 1/4 tsp pepper
- 1/2 tsp salt

Directions:

1. Place the inner pot in the PowerXL grill air fryer combo base.
2. Place pork chops into the inner pot.
3. Pour remaining ingredients over the pork chops.
4. Cover the inner pot with a glass lid.
5. Select slow cook mode then press the temperature button and set the time for 6 hours. Press start.
6. When the timer reaches 0, then press the cancel button.
7. Serve and enjoy.

Nutritional Value (Amount per Serving):

- Calories 401
- Fat 28.6 g
- Carbohydrates 7.3 g
- Sugar 4.3 g
- Protein 28.2 g
- Cholesterol 98 mg

Lamb Patties

Preparation Time: 10 minutes
Cooking Time: 15 minutes
Serve: 4

Ingredients:

- 1 lb ground lamb
- 1/4 cup fresh parsley, chopped
- 1/4 cup onion, minced
- 1/4 tsp cayenne pepper
- 1 tsp ground coriander
- 1/2 tsp ground allspice
- 1 tbsp garlic, minced
- 1 tsp ground cumin
- 1/4 tsp pepper
- 1 tsp ground cinnamon
- 1 tsp kosher salt

Directions:

1. Place the inner pot in the PowerXL grill air fryer combo base.
2. Add all ingredients into the large bowl and mix until well combined.
3. Make small balls from the meat mixture and place them into the inner pot.
4. Cover the inner pot with an air frying lid.
5. Select bake mode then set the temperature to 450 F and time for 15 minutes. Press start.
6. When the timer reaches 0, then press the cancel button.
7. Serve and enjoy.

Nutritional Value (Amount per Serving):

- Calories 223
- Fat 8.5 g
- Carbohydrates 2.6 g
- Sugar 0.4 g
- Protein 32.3 g
- Cholesterol 102 mg

Tasty Flank Steak

Preparation Time: 10 minutes
Cooking Time: 9 hours
Serve: 6

Ingredients:

- 1 1/2 lbs flank steak
- 2 bell pepper, sliced
- 1 1/2 tsp chili powder
- 15 oz salsa
- 3 garlic cloves, minced
- 1 onion, chopped
- 1/4 tsp pepper
- 1/2 tsp salt

Directions:

1. Add all ingredients into the large zip-lock bag and mix well.
2. Place a zip-lock bag into the refrigerator overnight.
3. Add marinated steak into the inner pot.
4. Place the inner pot in the PowerXL grill air fryer combo base.
5. Cover the inner pot with a glass lid.
6. Select slow cook mode then press the temperature button and set the time for 9 hours. Press start.
7. When the timer reaches 0, then press the cancel button.
8. Slice and serve.

Nutritional Value (Amount per Serving):

- Calories 264
- Fat 9.8 g
- Carbohydrates 10.1 g
- Sugar 5 g
- Protein 33.4 g
- Cholesterol 62 mg

Curried Pork Chops

Preparation Time: 10 minutes
Cooking Time: 6 hours
Serve: 8

Ingredients:

- 2 lbs pork chops
- 1 tbsp dried rosemary
- 1/4 cup olive oil
- 1 tbsp ground cumin
- 1 tbsp fresh chives, chopped
- 1 tbsp curry powder
- 1 tbsp dried thyme
- 1 tbsp fennel seeds
- 1 tsp salt

Directions:

1. Place the inner pot in the PowerXL grill air fryer combo base.
2. In a small bowl, mix cumin, rosemary, 2 tbsp oil, fennel seeds, chives, curry powder, thyme, and salt and rub over pork chops.
3. Place pork chops into the inner pot.
4. Pour remaining olive oil over pork chops.
5. Cover the inner pot with a glass lid.
6. Select slow cook mode then press the temperature button and set the time for 6 hours. Press start.
7. When the timer reaches 0, then press the cancel button.
8. Serve and enjoy.

Nutritional Value (Amount per Serving):

- Calories 427
- Fat 35 g
- Carbohydrates 1.7 g
- Sugar 0.1 g
- Protein 25.9 g
- Cholesterol 98 mg

Flavorful Beef Curry

Preparation Time: 10 minutes
Cooking Time: 6 hours
Serve: 2

Ingredients:

- 1 lb beef stew meat, cut into cubed
- 1/2 tbsp fresh ginger, minced
- 1/2 tsp cumin
- 1 tbsp curry powder
- 1/2 lb small red potatoes, cut into quarters
- 15 oz can roasted tomatoes, diced
- 1 garlic clove, minced
- 1/4 tsp black pepper
- 1/2 tsp salt

Directions:

1. Place the inner pot in the PowerXL grill air fryer combo base.
2. Add all ingredients into the inner pot and mix well.
3. Cover the inner pot with a glass lid.
4. Select slow cook mode then press the temperature button and set the time for 6 hours. Press start.
5. When the timer reaches 0, then press the cancel button.
6. Serve and enjoy.

Nutritional Value (Amount per Serving):

- Calories 521
- Fat 15 g
- Carbohydrates 21.7 g
- Sugar 1.3 g
- Protein 71.7 g
- Cholesterol 203 mg

Beef Bean Chili

Preparation Time: 10 minutes
Cooking Time: 6 hours
Serve: 2

Ingredients:

- 1 cup ground beef, cooked
- 2 tbsp dry onion, minced
- 15 oz can tomato sauce
- 15 oz can pinto beans, drained
- 1 packet taco seasoning mix

Directions:

1. Place the inner pot in the PowerXL grill air fryer combo base.
2. Add all ingredients into the inner pot and mix well.
3. Cover the inner pot with a glass lid.
4. Select slow cook mode then press the temperature button and set the time for 6 hours. Press start.
5. When the timer reaches 0, then press the cancel button.
6. Serve and enjoy.

Nutritional Value (Amount per Serving):

- Calories 658
- Fat 9.4 g
- Carbohydrates 87.2 g
- Sugar 9.5 g
- Protein 58.4 g
- Cholesterol 101 mg

Flavorful Beef Chili

Preparation Time: 10 minutes
Cooking Time: 6 hours
Serve: 2

Ingredients:

- 1/2 lb ground beef
- 1 tbsp chili powder
- 15 oz chili sauce
- 1/2 small onion, diced
- 8 oz can tomato sauce
- 1 tsp parsley
- 1/4 tsp cumin
- 1/8 cup steak sauce
- 1/4 tsp salt

Directions:

1. Place the inner pot in the PowerXL grill air fryer combo base.
2. Add all ingredients into the inner pot and mix well.
3. Cover the inner pot with a glass lid.
4. Select slow cook mode then press the temperature button and set the time for 6 hours. Press start.
5. When the timer reaches 0, then press the cancel button.
6. Serve and enjoy.

Nutritional Value (Amount per Serving):

- Calories 441
- Fat 8.8 g
- Carbohydrates 53.7 g
- Sugar 32.5 g
- Protein 38.5 g
- Cholesterol 101 mg

Chapter 6: Fish & Seafood

Lime Cajun Salmon

Preparation Time: 10 minutes
Cooking Time: 12 minutes
Serve: 1

Ingredients:

- 1 lb salmon fillets
- 3 tbsp olive oil
- 1/4 cup parsley, minced
- 1 lime juice
- 2 tsp Cajun seasonings
- 1/8 tsp cayenne pepper
- 1 tsp paprika
- 2 tsp onion powder
- 2 tsp garlic powder
- Pepper
- Salt

Directions:

1. In a small bowl, mix together Cajun seasoning, pepper, garlic powder, onion powder, paprika, cayenne pepper, and salt.
2. Brush fillets with oil and rub with spice mixture.
3. Place fish fillets in a baking dish. Pour lime juice over fish fillets.
4. Place the inner pot in the PowerXL grill air fryer combo base.
5. Place baking dish into the inner pot.
6. Cover the inner pot with an air frying lid.
7. Select bake mode then set the temperature to 475 F and time for 12 minutes. Press start.
8. When the timer reaches 0, then press the cancel button.
9. Garnish with parsley and serve.

Nutritional Value (Amount per Serving):

- Calories 1019
- Fat 70.6 g
- Carbohydrates 14 g
- Sugar 4.2 g
- Protein 90.5 g
- Cholesterol 200 mg

Salmon Casserole

Preparation Time: 10 minutes
Cooking Time: 45 minutes
Serve: 6

Ingredients:

- 2 cups elbow macaroni
- 5 oz milk
- 10.5 oz can cream of celery soup
- 14.75 oz can salmon, drained, bones & skin removed, cut into chunks
- 1 cup crackers, crushed
- 2 tbsp butter, melted
- 1 cup cheddar cheese, grated

Directions:

1. Cook macaroni according to the packet instructions. Drain well and set aside.
2. In a mixing bowl, mix together macaroni, salmon, cream of celery soup, milk, and cheese.
3. Pour macaroni mixture into the baking dish.
4. Mix together melted butter and crushed crackers and sprinkle over macaroni mixture.
5. Place the inner pot in the PowerXL grill air fryer combo base.
6. Place baking dish into the inner pot.
7. Cover the inner pot with an air frying lid.
8. Select bake mode then set the temperature to 350 F and time for 45 minutes. Press start.
9. When the timer reaches 0, then press the cancel button.
10. Serve and enjoy.

Nutritional Value (Amount per Serving):

- Calories 429
- Fat 20.9 g
- Carbohydrates 32.1 g
- Sugar 2.8 g
- Protein 26.8 g
- Cholesterol 68 mg

Lime Garlic Cod

Preparation Time: 10 minutes
Cooking Time: 20 minutes
Serve: 4

Ingredients:

- 1 1/2 lb cod fillet
- 1 lime, sliced
- 1/4 cup butter, diced
- 2 lemon juice
- 2 tbsp olive oil
- 4 garlic cloves, minced
- Pepper
- Salt

Directions:

1. Place cod fillet in the baking dish and season with pepper and salt.
2. Whisk together garlic, lime juice, and olive oil and pour over cod.
3. Arrange butter pieces and lemon slices on top of cod.
4. Place the inner pot in the PowerXL grill air fryer combo base.
5. Place baking dish into the inner pot.
6. Cover the inner pot with an air frying lid.
7. Select bake mode then set the temperature to 390 F and time for 20 minutes. Press start.
8. When the timer reaches 0, then press the cancel button.
9. Serve and enjoy.

Nutritional Value (Amount per Serving):

- Calories 309
- Fat 20.3 g
- Carbohydrates 1.7 g
- Sugar 0.6 g
- Protein 30.9 g
- Cholesterol 114 mg

Greek Salmon

Preparation Time: 10 minutes
Cooking Time: 30 minutes
Serve: 6

Ingredients:

- 2 1/2 lbs salmon fillet
- 4 tbsp olive oil
- 1 small onion, sliced
- 2 tsp capers
- 1 3/4 cups cherry tomatoes, halved
- 1/2 tsp oregano, chopped
- 1/2 cup olives pitted
- 2 lemons, sliced
- 1/2 tsp fresh thyme, chopped
- 1/2 tsp rosemary, chopped
- Pepper
- Salt

Directions:

1. Place salmon fillet on a baking dish.
2. Arrange lemon slices and onions, capers, olives, and tomatoes around the salmon.
3. Drizzle salmon with oil and season with pepper and salt.
4. Place the inner pot in the PowerXL grill air fryer combo base.
5. Place baking dish into the inner pot.
6. Cover the inner pot with an air frying lid.
7. Select bake mode then set the temperature to 425 F and time for 30 minutes. Press start.
8. When the timer reaches 0, then press the cancel button.
9. Garnish with herbs and serve.

Nutritional Value (Amount per Serving):

- Calories 362
- Fat 23 g
- Carbohydrates 5 g
- Sugar 2.3 g
- Protein 36 g
- Cholesterol 82 mg

Scallop Gratin

Preparation Time: 10 minutes
Cooking Time: 8 minutes
Serve: 4

Ingredients:

- 1 1/2 lbs sea scallops
- 1 lemon juice
- 1/4 cup white wine
- 1/4 cup cream cheese, softened
- 1/4 cup parmesan cheese, shaved
- Pepper
- Salt

Directions:

1. Add scallops to the baking dish.
2. In a bowl, whisk together lemon juice, cream cheese, white wine, tarragon, parmesan cheese, pepper, and salt and pour over scallops.
3. Place the inner pot in the PowerXL grill air fryer combo base.
4. Place baking dish into the inner pot.
5. Cover the inner pot with an air frying lid.
6. Select bake mode then set the temperature to 390 F and time for 8 minutes. Press start.
7. When the timer reaches 0, then press the cancel button.
8. Serve and enjoy.

Nutritional Value (Amount per Serving):

- Calories 235
- Fat 7.7 g
- Carbohydrates 5.5 g
- Sugar 0.4 g
- Protein 31.6 g
- Cholesterol 76 mg

Sweet Orange Salmon

Preparation Time: 10 minutes
Cooking Time: 25 minutes
Serve: 2

Ingredients:

- 1 lb salmon fillets
- 1 orange juice
- 1 orange zest, grated
- 2 tbsp honey
- 3 tbsp soy sauce

Directions:

1. In a small bowl, whisk together honey, soy sauce, orange juice, and orange zest.
2. Place salmon fillets in a baking dish and pour honey mixture over salmon fillets.
3. Place the inner pot in the PowerXL grill air fryer combo base.
4. Place baking dish into the inner pot.
5. Cover the inner pot with an air frying lid.
6. Select bake mode then set the temperature to 425 F and time for 25 minutes. Press start.
7. When the timer reaches 0, then press the cancel button.
8. Serve and enjoy.

Nutritional Value (Amount per Serving):

- Calories 399
- Fat 14.1 g
- Carbohydrates 24.4 g
- Sugar 21.3 g
- Protein 45.9 g
- Cholesterol 100 mg

Lemon Pepper Basa

Preparation Time: 10 minutes
Cooking Time: 12 minutes
Serve: 4

Ingredients:

- 4 basa fish fillets
- 1/4 tsp lemon pepper seasoning
- 4 tbsp fresh lemon juice
- 1/4 cup green onion, sliced
- 1/2 tsp garlic powder
- 8 tsp olive oil
- Pepper
- Salt

Directions:

1. Place fish fillets in a baking dish and spray with cooking spray.
2. Pour oil and lemon juice over fish fillets. Sprinkle remaining ingredients over fish fillets.
3. Place the inner pot in the PowerXL grill air fryer combo base.
4. Place baking dish into the inner pot.
5. Cover the inner pot with an air frying lid.
6. Select bake mode then set the temperature to 425 F and time for 12 minutes. Press start.
7. When the timer reaches 0, then press the cancel button.
8. Serve and enjoy.

Nutritional Value (Amount per Serving):

- Calories 307
- Fat 21.4 g
- Carbohydrates 5.3 g
- Sugar 3.4 g
- Protein 24 g
- Cholesterol 0 mg

Buttery Scallops

Preparation Time: 10 minutes
Cooking Time: 15 minutes
Serve: 4

Ingredients:

- 1 1/2 lbs sea scallops
- 4 tbsp parmesan cheese, grated
- 1/2 cup breadcrumbs
- 1/4 tsp paprika
- 1/8 tsp cayenne
- 2 tbsp olive oil
- 4 tbsp butter, melted
- Pepper
- Salt

Directions:

1. Add scallops to the baking dish.
2. Mix together breadcrumbs, cayenne, paprika, parmesan cheese, parsley, butter, oil, pepper, and salt and spread over scallops.
3. Place the inner pot in the PowerXL grill air fryer combo base.
4. Place baking dish into the inner pot.
5. Cover the inner pot with an air frying lid.
6. Select bake mode then set the temperature to 390 F and time for 15 minutes. Press start.
7. When the timer reaches 0, then press the cancel button.
8. Serve and enjoy.

Nutritional Value (Amount per Serving):

- Calories 384
- Fat 21.8 g
- Carbohydrates 14.2 g
- Sugar 0.9 g
- Protein 32.4 g
- Cholesterol 91 mg

Delicious Pesto Salmon

Preparation Time: 10 minutes
Cooking Time: 20 minutes
Serve: 4

Ingredients:

- 4 salmon fillets
- 7 tbsp feta cheese, crumbled
- 1 3/4 cups cherry tomatoes, halved
- 1 onion, chopped
- 1/2 cup pesto

Directions:

1. Place salmon fillet in baking dish.
2. Add tomatoes, onion, pesto, and cheese on top of each salmon fillet.
3. Place the inner pot in the PowerXL grill air fryer combo base.
4. Place baking dish into the inner pot.
5. Cover the inner pot with an air frying lid.
6. Select bake mode then set the temperature to 350 F and time for 20 minutes. Press start.
7. When the timer reaches 0, then press the cancel button.
8. Serve and enjoy.

Nutritional Value (Amount per Serving):

- Calories 446
- Fat 28 g
- Carbohydrates 9 g
- Sugar 6 g
- Protein 41 g
- Cholesterol 103 mg

Baked Catfish

Preparation Time: 10 minutes
Cooking Time: 15 minutes
Serve: 4

Ingredients:

- 1 lb catfish fillets, cut 1/2-inch thick
- 2 tsp onion powder
- 1 tbsp dried oregano, crushed
- 1/2 tsp ground cumin
- 3/4 tsp chili powder
- 1 tsp crushed red pepper
- Pepper
- Salt

Directions:

1. In a small bowl, mix together cumin, chili powder, crushed red pepper, onion powder, oregano, pepper, and salt.
2. Rub fish fillets with the spice mixture on both sides.
3. Place fish fillets in a baking dish.
4. Place the inner pot in the PowerXL grill air fryer combo base.
5. Place baking dish into the inner pot.
6. Cover the inner pot with an air frying lid.
7. Select bake mode then set the temperature to 350 F and time for 15 minutes. Press start.
8. When the timer reaches 0, then press the cancel button.
9. Serve and enjoy.

Nutritional Value (Amount per Serving):

- Calories 165
- Fat 9 g
- Carbohydrates 2.4 g
- Sugar 0.6 g
- Protein 18 g
- Cholesterol 53 mg

Italian Halibut

Preparation Time: 10 minutes
Cooking Time: 15 minutes
Serve: 2

Ingredients:

- 1 lb halibut
- 1 tsp garlic, minced
- 2 tbsp mayonnaise
- 2 tbsp sun-dried tomatoes, chopped
- 1 1/2 tbsp fresh basil, chopped
- 1/4 tsp dried oregano
- Pepper
- Salt

Directions:

1. In a small bowl, mix together sun-dried tomatoes, oregano, garlic, and mayonnaise.
2. Place fish skin side down in prepared baking dish. Season with pepper and salt.
3. Spread tomato mixture on top of fish.
4. Place the inner pot in the PowerXL grill air fryer combo base.
5. Place baking dish into the inner pot.
6. Cover the inner pot with an air frying lid.
7. Select bake mode then set the temperature to 425 F and time for 15 minutes. Press start.
8. When the timer reaches 0, then press the cancel button.
9. Garnish with basil and serve.

Nutritional Value (Amount per Serving):

- Calories 301
- Fat 10 g
- Carbohydrates 4.6 g
- Sugar 1.3 g
- Protein 45.8 g
- Cholesterol 76 mg

Sweet & Spicy Cajun Salmon

Preparation Time: 10 minutes
Cooking Time: 12 minutes
Serve: 4

Ingredients:

- 4 salmon fillets
- 4 tbsp brown sugar
- 2 tsp Cajun seasoning

Directions:

1. Mix together Cajun seasoning and brown sugar and rub all over salmon.
2. Place salmon in a baking dish.
3. Place the inner pot in the PowerXL grill air fryer combo base.
4. Place baking dish into the inner pot.
5. Cover the inner pot with an air frying lid.
6. Select bake mode then set the temperature to 390 F and time for 12 minutes. Press start.
7. When the timer reaches 0, then press the cancel button.
8. Serve and enjoy.

Nutritional Value (Amount per Serving):

- Calories 270
- Fat 11 g
- Carbohydrates 8.8 g
- Sugar 8.7 g
- Protein 34.6 g
- Cholesterol 78 mg

Dijon Salmon

Preparation Time: 10 minutes
Cooking Time: 12 minutes
Serve: 4

Ingredients:

- 4 salmon fillets
- 3 tbsp maple syrup
- 2 tbsp ground Dijon mustard

Directions:

1. Arrange salmon fillets in a baking dish.
2. Mix together Dijon mustard and maple syrup and brush over salmon fillets.
3. Place the inner pot in the PowerXL grill air fryer combo base.
4. Place baking dish into the inner pot.
5. Cover the inner pot with an air frying lid.
6. Select bake mode then set the temperature to 390 F and time for 12 minutes. Press start.
7. When the timer reaches 0, then press the cancel button.
8. Serve and enjoy.

Nutritional Value (Amount per Serving):

- Calories 282
- Fat 11 g
- Carbohydrates 10.1 g
- Sugar 8.9 g
- Protein 34.5 g
- Cholesterol 78 mg

Baked Shrimp

Preparation Time: 10 minutes
Cooking Time: 12 minutes
Serve: 4

Ingredients:

- 1 1/4 lbs shrimp, peeled and deveined
- 1 tbsp garlic, minced
- 1/4 cup butter
- 2 tbsp fresh lemon juice
- Pepper
- Salt

Directions:

1. Place the inner pot in the PowerXL grill air fryer combo base.
2. Add all ingredients into the inner pot and mix well.
3. Cover the inner pot with an air frying lid.
4. Select bake mode then set the temperature to 350 F and time for 12 minutes. Press start.
5. When the timer reaches 0, then press the cancel button.
6. Serve and enjoy.

Nutritional Value (Amount per Serving):

- Calories 276
- Fat 14 g
- Carbohydrates 3.2 g
- Sugar 0.2 g
- Protein 32.7 g
- Cholesterol 329 mg

Dill White Fish Fillets

Preparation Time: 10 minutes
Cooking Time: 15 minutes
Serve: 4

Ingredients:

- 16 oz white fish fillets
- 2 tbsp fresh lime juice
- 1 tbsp Dijon mustard
- 1/2 tsp dried dill
- 1 tbsp olive oil
- 1/4 tsp pepper

Directions:

1. Place white fish fillets in the baking dish.
2. Mix together olive oil, lime juice, dill, Dijon mustard, and pepper and brush over fish fillets.
3. Place the inner pot in the PowerXL grill air fryer combo base.
4. Place baking dish into the inner pot.
5. Cover the inner pot with an air frying lid.
6. Select bake mode then set the temperature to 390 F and time for 15 minutes. Press start.
7. When the timer reaches 0, then press the cancel button.
8. Serve and enjoy.

Nutritional Value (Amount per Serving):

- Calories 230
- Fat 12.3 g
- Carbohydrates 0.5 g
- Sugar 0.2 g
- Protein 28 g
- Cholesterol 87 mg

Chapter 7: Vegetables & Side Dishes

Healthy Artichoke Casserole

Preparation Time: 10 minutes
Cooking Time: 30 minutes
Serve: 12

Ingredients:

- 16 eggs
- 14 oz can artichoke hearts, drained and cut into pieces
- 1/4 cup coconut milk
- 1/2 tsp red pepper, crushed
- 1/2 tsp thyme, diced
- 1/2 cup ricotta cheese
- 1/2 cup parmesan cheese
- 1 cup cheddar cheese, shredded
- 10 oz frozen spinach, thawed and drain well
- 1 garlic cloves, minced
- 1/4 cup onion, shaved
- 1 tsp salt

Directions:

1. In a large bowl, whisk together eggs and coconut milk.
2. Add spinach and artichoke into the egg mixture.
3. Add all remaining ingredients except ricotta cheese and stir well to combine.
4. Place the inner pot in the PowerXL grill air fryer combo base.
5. Pour egg mixture into the inner pot.
6. Spread ricotta cheese on top of the egg mixture.
7. Cover the inner pot with an air frying lid.
8. Select bake mode then set the temperature to 350 F and time for 30 minutes. Press start.
9. When the timer reaches 0, then press the cancel button.
10. Serve and enjoy.

Nutritional Value (Amount per Serving):

- Calories 205
- Fat 13.7 g
- Carbohydrates 4.9 g
- Sugar 1.5 g
- Protein 15.9 g
- Cholesterol 266 mg

Baked Cauliflower

Preparation Time: 10 minutes
Cooking Time: 45 minutes
Serve: 2

Ingredients:

- 1/2 cauliflower head, cut into florets
- 2 tbsp olive oil

For seasoning:

- 1/2 tsp white pepper
- 1/2 tsp garlic powder
- 1/2 tsp ground cumin
- 1/2 tsp black pepper
- 1 tbsp ground cayenne
- 1 tsp onion powder
- 1/4 tsp dried oregano
- 1/4 tsp dried basil
- 1/4 tsp dried thyme
- 2 tbsp ground paprika
- 2 tsp salt

Directions:

1. In a large bowl, mix together all seasoning ingredients.
2. Add oil and stir well. Add cauliflower to the bowl seasoning mixture and stir well to coat.
3. Place the inner pot in the PowerXL grill air fryer combo base.
4. Spread the cauliflower florets into the inner pot.
5. Cover the inner pot with an air frying lid.
6. Select bake mode then set the temperature to 400 F and time for 45 minutes. Press start.
7. When the timer reaches 0, then press the cancel button.
8. Serve and enjoy.

Nutritional Value (Amount per Serving):

- Calories 177
- Fat 15.6 g
- Carbohydrates 11.5 g
- Sugar 3.2 g
- Protein 3.1 g
- Cholesterol 0 mg

Red Beans Rice

Preparation Time: 10 minutes
Cooking Time: 8 hours
Serve: 8

Ingredients:

- 1 cup dried red beans, soaked overnight
- 1 1/2 cups rice, rinsed
- 1/2 tsp thyme
- 1 lime juice
- 2 cups of coconut milk
- 3 cups vegetable stock
- 2 garlic cloves, minced
- 1/4 tsp allspice
- 1 tsp red pepper flakes
- 1/2 tsp ground ginger
- 1/2 tsp salt

Directions:

1. Drain beans and place them into the large pot. Add fresh water and bring to boil for 10-15 minutes.
2. Place the inner pot in the PowerXL grill air fryer combo base.
3. Drain beans and add them into the inner pot.
4. Add remaining ingredients and stir well.
5. Cover the inner pot with a glass lid.
6. Select slow cook mode then press the temperature button and set the time for 8 hours. Press start.
7. When the timer reaches 0, then press the cancel button.
8. Serve and enjoy.

Nutritional Value (Amount per Serving):

- Calories 348
- Fat 14.9 g
- Carbohydrates 46.5 g
- Sugar 2.9 g
- Protein 9.3 g
- Cholesterol 0 mg

Delicious Carrot Tomato Soup

Preparation Time: 10 minutes
Cooking Time: 6 hours
Serve: 4

Ingredients:

- 14.5 oz can tomatoes, diced
- 4 medium carrots, peeled and chopped
- 1 tbsp turmeric
- 1 cup of coconut milk
- 1 tsp ground cumin
- 1 tsp ground coriander
- Pepper
- Salt

Directions:

1. Place the inner pot in the PowerXL grill air fryer combo base.
2. Add all ingredients into the inner pot and mix well.
3. Cover the inner pot with a glass lid.
4. Select slow cook mode then press the temperature button and set the time for 6 hours. Press start.
5. When the timer reaches 0, then press the cancel button.
6. Puree the soup using an immersion blender until smooth.
7. Season with pepper and salt.
8. Serve and enjoy.

Nutritional Value (Amount per Serving):

- Calories 193
- Fat 14.6 g
- Carbohydrates 15.9 g
- Sugar 8.6 g
- Protein 3 g
- Cholesterol 0 mg

Flavorful Ratatouille

Preparation Time: 10 minutes
Cooking Time: 4 hours
Serve: 8

Ingredients:

- 2 summer squash, sliced
- 1 bell pepper, chopped
- 1 eggplant, chopped
- 1 tbsp garlic, minced
- 1/4 tsp red pepper flakes
- 1 tsp dried oregano
- 2 tbsp tomato paste
- 1 cup cherry tomatoes, chopped
- 1 onion, chopped
- 1 cup fresh basil, chopped
- 2 tbsp olive oil
- 1/4 tsp pepper
- 1/2 tsp sea salt

Directions:

1. Place the inner pot in the PowerXL grill air fryer combo base.
2. Add all ingredients into the inner pot and mix well.
3. Cover the inner pot with a glass lid.
4. Select slow cook mode then press the temperature button and set the time for 4 hours. Press start.
5. When the timer reaches 0, then press the cancel button.
6. Serve and enjoy.

Nutritional Value (Amount per Serving):

- Calories 71
- Fat 3.9 g
- Carbohydrates 9.3 g
- Sugar 5.3 g
- Protein 1.8 g
- Cholesterol 0 mg

Curried Tomato Soup

Preparation Time: 10 minutes
Cooking Time: 6 hours
Serve: 8

Ingredients:

- 4 lbs tomatoes, cored and diced
- 2 tbsp onion, minced
- 1 tsp garlic, minced
- 2 tsp curry powder
- 2 cups of coconut milk
- 1 cup of water
- 1 tsp salt

Directions:

1. Place the inner pot in the PowerXL grill air fryer combo base.
2. Add all ingredients into the inner pot and stir well.
3. Cover the inner pot with a glass lid.
4. Select slow cook mode then press the temperature button and set the time for 6 hours. Press start.
5. When the timer reaches 0, then press the cancel button.
6. Puree the soup using a blender until smooth.
7. Stir well and serve.

Nutritional Value (Amount per Serving):

- Calories 182
- Fat 14.8 g
- Carbohydrates 12 g
- Sugar 8.1 g
- Protein 3.5 g
- Cholesterol 0 mg

Three Bean Chili

Preparation Time: 10 minutes
Cooking Time: 4 hours
Serve: 6

Ingredients:

- 28 oz can red beans, drained
- 14 oz can black beans, drained
- 1 tsp cumin
- 1 cup of salsa
- 2 1/2 cups vegetable stock
- 2 garlic cloves, minced
- 1 small onion, diced
- 1 tsp cayenne
- 14 oz can tomato, diced
- 14 oz can pinto beans, drained
- 1 1/2 cups frozen corn, defrosted
- 2 bell peppers, diced
- Pepper
- Salt

Directions:

1. Place the inner pot in the PowerXL grill air fryer combo base.
2. Add all ingredients into the inner pot and stir well.
3. Cover the inner pot with a glass lid.
4. Select slow cook mode then press the temperature button and set the time for 4 hours. Press start.
5. When the timer reaches 0, then press the cancel button.
6. Serve and enjoy.

Nutritional Value (Amount per Serving):

- Calories 352
- Fat 1.7 g
- Carbohydrates 65.7 g
- Sugar 9.6 g
- Protein 19.4 g
- Cholesterol 0 mg

Tomato Green Bean Soup

Preparation Time: 10 minutes
Cooking Time: 6 hours
Serve: 8

Ingredients:

- 1 lb fresh green beans, cut into 1-inch pieces
- 1 cup carrots, chopped
- 3 cups fresh tomatoes, diced
- 1 garlic clove, minced
- 6 cups vegetable broth
- 1/4 tsp black pepper
- 1 cup onions, chopped
- 1 tsp basil, dried
- 1/2 tsp salt

Directions:

1. Place the inner pot in the PowerXL grill air fryer combo base.
2. Add all ingredients into the inner pot and stir well.
3. Cover the inner pot with a glass lid.
4. Select slow cook mode then press the temperature button and set the time for 6 hours. Press start.
5. When the timer reaches 0, then press the cancel button.
6. Serve and enjoy.

Nutritional Value (Amount per Serving):

- Calories 71
- Fat 1.3 g
- Carbohydrates 10.2 g
- Sugar 4.4 g
- Protein 5.6 g
- Cholesterol 0 mg

Creamy Cauliflower Casserole

Preparation Time: 10 minutes
Cooking Time: 15 minutes
Serve: 6

Ingredients:

- 1 cauliflower head, cut into florets, and boil
- 2 cups cheddar cheese, shredded
- 2 tsp Dijon mustard
- 2 oz cream cheese
- 1 cup heavy cream
- 1 tsp garlic powder
- 1/2 tsp pepper
- 1/2 tsp salt

Directions:

1. Place the inner pot in the PowerXL grill air fryer combo base.
2. Add all ingredients into the inner pot and mix well.
3. Cover the inner pot with an air frying lid.
4. Select bake mode then set the temperature to 375 F and time for 15 minutes. Press start.
5. When the timer reaches 0, then press the cancel button.
6. Serve and enjoy.

Nutritional Value (Amount per Serving):

- Calories 268
- Fat 23.3 g
- Carbohydrates 4.2 g
- Sugar 1.4 g
- Protein 11.5 g
- Cholesterol 77 mg

Stuffed Pepper

Preparation Time: 10 minutes
Cooking Time: 25 minutes
Serve: 4

Ingredients:

- 4 eggs
- 1/4 cup baby broccoli florets
- 1/4 cup cherry tomatoes
- 1 tsp dried sage
- 2.5 oz cheddar cheese, grated
- 7 oz almond milk
- 2 bell peppers, cut in half and deseeded
- Pepper
- Salt

Directions:

1. In a bowl, whisk together eggs, milk, broccoli, cherry tomatoes, sage, pepper, and salt.
2. Pour egg mixture into the bell pepper halves.
3. Sprinkle cheese on top of bell pepper.
4. Place the inner pot in the PowerXL grill air fryer combo base.
5. Place stuffed peppers into the inner pot.
6. Cover the inner pot with an air frying lid.
7. Select bake mode then set the temperature to 390 F and time for 25 minutes. Press start.
8. When the timer reaches 0, then press the cancel button.
9. Serve and enjoy.

Nutritional Value (Amount per Serving):

- Calories 285
- Fat 25.2 g
- Carbohydrates 5.8 g
- Sugar 3.3 g
- Protein 11.5 g
- Cholesterol 167 mg

Baked Eggplant & Zucchini

Preparation Time: 10 minutes
Cooking Time: 35 minutes
Serve: 6

Ingredients:

- 1 medium eggplant, sliced
- 3 medium zucchini, sliced
- 3 oz Parmesan cheese, grated
- 4 tbsp parsley, chopped
- 4 tbsp basil, chopped
- 1 tbsp olive oil
- 4 garlic cloves, minced
- 1 cup cherry tomatoes, halved
- 1/4 tsp pepper
- 1/4 tsp salt

Directions:

1. In a mixing bowl, add cherry tomatoes, eggplant, zucchini, olive oil, garlic, cheese, basil, pepper, and salt toss well until combined.
2. Transfer the eggplant mixture into the greased baking dish.
3. Place the inner pot in the PowerXL grill air fryer combo base.
4. Place baking dish into the inner pot.
5. Cover the inner pot with an air frying lid.
6. Select bake mode then set the temperature to 350 F and time for 35 minutes. Press start.
7. When the timer reaches 0, then press the cancel button.
8. Garnish with chopped parsley and serve.

Nutritional Value (Amount per Serving):

- Calories 110
- Fat 5.8 g
- Carbohydrates 10.4 g
- Sugar 4.8 g
- Protein 7.0 g
- Cholesterol 10 mg

Mushroom Barley Soup

Preparation Time: 10 minutes
Cooking Time: 8 hours
Serve: 8

Ingredients:

- 2/3 cup pearl barley
- 16 oz button mushrooms, sliced
- 1 large onion, diced
- 6 cups vegetable broth
- 1 garlic clove, minced
- 1/4 tsp pepper
- 1/2 tsp salt

Directions:

1. Place the inner pot in the PowerXL grill air fryer combo base.
2. Add all ingredients into the inner pot and mix well.
3. Cover the inner pot with a glass lid.
4. Select slow cook mode then press the temperature button and set the time for 8 hours. Press start.
5. When the timer reaches 0, then press the cancel button.
6. Serve and enjoy.

Nutritional Value (Amount per Serving):

- Calories 108
- Fat 1.4 g
- Carbohydrates 17.4 g
- Sugar 2.4 g
- Protein 7.3 g
- Cholesterol 0 mg

Easy Baked Beans

Preparation Time: 10 minutes
Cooking Time: 10 minutes
Serve: 2

Ingredients:

- 16 oz can white beans, drained and rinsed
- 2 tbsp BBQ sauce
- 1 1/2 tbsp maple syrup
- 1 1/2 tsp lemon juice
- 1 tbsp prepared yellow mustard

Directions:

1. Place the inner pot in the PowerXL grill air fryer combo base.
2. Add all ingredients into the inner pot and stir well.
3. Cover the inner pot with a glass lid.
4. Select simmer mode then presses the temperature button and set the time for 10 minutes. Press start.
5. When the timer reaches 0, then press the cancel button.
6. Stir well and serve.

Nutritional Value (Amount per Serving):

- Calories 278
- Fat 0.4 g
- Carbohydrates 52.9 g
- Sugar 14.9 g
- Protein 14.3 g
- Cholesterol 0 mg

Scalloped Potatoes

Preparation Time: 10 minutes
Cooking Time: 45 minutes
Serve: 6

Ingredients:

- 4 sweet potatoes, peeled
- 1/4 cup olive oil
- 1/2 tsp paprika
- 1 tbsp maple syrup
- 1/2 cup fresh orange juice
- 1/2 tsp orange zest
- 1 tsp salt

Directions:

1. Slice sweet potatoes 1/16-inch thick using a slicer.
2. Arrange sweet potato slices into the greased baking dish.
3. In a bowl, whisk together the remaining ingredients and pour over sweet potatoes.
4. Place the inner pot in the PowerXL grill air fryer combo base.
5. Place baking dish into the inner pot.
6. Cover the inner pot with an air frying lid.
7. Select bake mode then set the temperature to 350 F and time for 45 minutes. Press start.
8. When the timer reaches 0, then press the cancel button.
9. Serve and enjoy.

Nutritional Value (Amount per Serving):

- Calories 91
- Fat 8.6 g
- Carbohydrates 32.4 g
- Sugar 4.2 g
- Protein 1.7 g
- Cholesterol 0 mg

Mac & Cheese

Preparation Time: 10 minutes
Cooking Time: 20 minutes
Serve: 10

Ingredients:

- 1 lb cooked macaroni
- 1/2 cup breadcrumbs
- 12 oz cheddar cheese, shredded
- 4 1/2 cups milk
- 1/2 cup flour
- 1/2 cup butter
- Pepper
- Salt

Directions:

1. Place the inner pot in the PowerXL grill air fryer combo base.
2. Add all ingredients except breadcrumbs into the inner pot and mix well. Sprinkle breadcrumbs on top.
3. Cover the inner pot with an air frying lid.
4. Select bake mode then set the temperature to 350 F and time for 20 minutes. Press start.
5. When the timer reaches 0, then press the cancel button.
6. Serve and enjoy.

Nutritional Value (Amount per Serving):

- Calories 486
- Fat 23.8 g
- Carbohydrates 48.4 g
- Sugar 6.7 g
- Protein 19.5 g
- Cholesterol 69 mg

Healthy Broccoli Casserole

Preparation Time: 10 minutes
Cooking Time: 30 minutes
Serve: 6

Ingredients:

- 15 oz broccoli florets
- 10 oz can cream of mushroom soup
- 1 cup mozzarella cheese, shredded
- 1/3 cup milk
- 1/2 tsp onion powder

For topping:

- 1 tbsp butter, melted
- 1/2 cup crushed crackers

Directions:

1. Place the inner pot in the PowerXL grill air fryer combo base.
2. Add all ingredients except topping ingredients into the inner pot.
3. In a small bowl, mix together cracker crumbs and melted butter and sprinkle over the inner pot mixture.
4. Cover the inner pot with an air frying lid.
5. Select bake mode then set the temperature to 350 F and time for 30 minutes. Press start.
6. When the timer reaches 0, then press the cancel button.
7. Serve and enjoy.

Nutritional Value (Amount per Serving):

- Calories 179
- Fat 10.6 g
- Carbohydrates 11.8 g
- Sugar 3.7 g
- Protein 7 g
- Cholesterol 27 mg

Baked Tomato

Preparation Time: 10 minutes
Cooking Time: 30 minutes
Serve: 2

Ingredients:

- 2 eggs
- 2 large fresh tomatoes
- 1 tsp fresh parsley
- Pepper
- Salt

Directions:

1. Cut off the top of a tomato and spoon out the tomato innards.
2. Break the egg in each tomato.
3. Place the inner pot in the PowerXL grill air fryer combo base.
4. Place tomato into the inner pot.
5. Cover the inner pot with an air frying lid.
6. Select bake mode then set the temperature to 350 F and time for 15 minutes. Press start.
7. When the timer reaches 0, then press the cancel button.
8. Season tomato with parsley, pepper, and salt.
9. Serve and enjoy.

Nutritional Value (Amount per Serving):

- Calories 96
- Fat 4.7 g
- Carbohydrates 7.5 g
- Sugar 5.1 g
- Protein 7.2 g
- Cholesterol 164 mg

Slow Cooked Vegetables

Preparation Time: 10 minutes
Cooking Time: 5 hours
Serve: 6

Ingredients:

- 1 lb eggplant, peeled and cut 1-inch cubes
- 1 zucchini, chopped
- 3 fresh tomatoes, diced
- 1/2 onion, diced
- 1 red bell pepper, chopped
- 1 tbsp olive oil
- 3 oz feta cheese, crumbled
- 2 tsp dried basil
- 1 tbsp garlic, minced
- Pepper
- Salt

Directions:

1. Place the inner pot in the PowerXL grill air fryer combo base.
2. Add all ingredients except feta cheese into the inner pot and stir well.
3. Cover the inner pot with a glass lid.
4. Select slow cook mode then press the temperature button and set the time for 5 hours. Press start.
5. When the timer reaches 0, then press the cancel button.
6. Top with crumbled cheese and serve.

Nutritional Value (Amount per Serving):

- Calories 105
- Fat 5.7 g
- Carbohydrates 11.4 g
- Sugar 6.4 g
- Protein 4.1 g
- Cholesterol 13 mg

Barley Risotto

Preparation Time: 10 minutes
Cooking Time: 6 hours
Serve: 4

Ingredients:

- 1 cup pearl barley
- 2 1/2 cups fresh spinach, chopped
- 1 onion, chopped
- 2 1/2 cups vegetable stock
- 2 garlic cloves, chopped
- Pepper
- Salt

Directions:

1. Place the inner pot in the PowerXL grill air fryer combo base.
2. Add barley, stock, garlic, and onion into the inner pot and mix well.
3. Cover the inner pot with a glass lid.
4. Select slow cook mode then press the temperature button and set the time for 6 hours. Press start.
5. When the timer reaches 0, then press the cancel button.
6. Stir in spinach. Season with pepper and salt.
7. Serve and enjoy.

Nutritional Value (Amount per Serving):

- Calories 197
- Fat 0.8 g
- Carbohydrates 43.2 g
- Sugar 2.1 g
- Protein 6.2 g
- Cholesterol 0 mg

Bean Stew

Preparation Time: 10 minutes
Cooking Time: 10 minutes
Serve: 6

Ingredients:

- 3 cups cooked red beans
- 1/3 cup bell peppers, diced
- 1/3 cup onion, diced
- 1/2 cup vegetable broth
- 1 tbsp olive oil
- 1/4 tsp kosher salt

Directions:

1. Place the inner pot in the PowerXL grill air fryer combo base.
2. Select saute mode and press start.
3. Add olive oil into the inner pot and heat the oil.
4. Add bell pepper and onion and sauté until onion is softened.
5. Press the cancel button.
6. Add broth, beans, and salt and stir well.
7. Cover the inner pot with a glass lid.
8. Select simmer mode then presses the temperature button and set the time for 10 minutes. Press start.
9. When the timer reaches 0, then press the cancel button.
10. Serve and enjoy.

Nutritional Value (Amount per Serving):

- Calories 338
- Fat 3.5 g
- Carbohydrates 57.6 g
- Sugar 2.6 g
- Protein 21.3 g
- Cholesterol 0 mg

Chapter 8: Snacks & Appetizers

Sweet Potato Bites

Preparation Time: 10 minutes
Cooking Time: 15 minutes
Serve: 2

Ingredients:

- 2 sweet potato, diced into 1-inch cubes
- 1 1/2 tsp cinnamon
- 2 tbsp olive oil
- 2 tbsp honey
- 1 tsp red chili flakes

Directions:

1. Add all ingredients into the bowl and toss well.
2. Place the inner pot in the PowerXL grill air fryer combo base.
3. Place grill plate in the inner pot. Cover.
4. Select air fry mode then set the temperature to 350 F and time for 15 minutes. Press start.
5. Let the appliance preheat for 3 minutes.
6. Open the lid then place sweet potato mixture on the grill plate.
7. Cover the inner pot with an air frying lid. Press start.
8. When the timer reaches 0, then press the cancel button.
9. Serve and enjoy.

Nutritional Value (Amount per Serving):

- Calories 291
- Fat 14.2 g
- Carbohydrates 42.3 g
- Sugar 24.7 g
- Protein 2.4 g
- Cholesterol 0 mg

Tofu Bites

Preparation Time: 10 minutes
Cooking Time: 20 minutes
Serve: 4

Ingredients:

- 1 block firm tofu, cut into 1-inch cubes
- 1 tsp vinegar
- 2 tbsp soy sauce
- 1 tbsp cornstarch
- 2 tsp sesame oil

Directions:

1. Add tofu, sesame oil, vinegar, and soy sauce in a large bowl and let marinate for 20 minutes.
2. Toss marinated tofu with cornstarch.
3. Place the inner pot in the PowerXL grill air fryer combo base.
4. Place grill plate in the inner pot. Cover.
5. Select air fry mode then set the temperature to 370 F and time for 20 minutes. Press start.
6. Let the appliance preheat for 3 minutes.
7. Open the lid then place tofu on the grill plate.
8. Cover the inner pot with an air frying lid. Press start.
9. When the timer reaches 0, then press the cancel button.
10. Serve and enjoy.

Nutritional Value (Amount per Serving):

- Calories 48
- Fat 3.2 g
- Carbohydrates 2.8 g
- Sugar 0.3 g
- Protein 2.4 g
- Cholesterol 0 mg

Veggie Fritters

Preparation Time: 10 minutes
Cooking Time: 15 minutes
Serve: 2

Ingredients:

- 1 egg, lightly beaten
- 1 1/2 cups frozen vegetable, steam & mashed
- 1/4 cup parmesan cheese, shredded
- 1/2 tbsp coconut flour
- 1/4 tsp garlic powder
- Pepper
- Salt

Directions:

1. Add all ingredients into the bowl and mix until well combined.
2. Make patties from the mixture.
3. Place the inner pot in the PowerXL grill air fryer combo base.
4. Place grill plate in the inner pot. Cover.
5. Select air fry mode then set the temperature to 390 F and time for 15 minutes. Press start.
6. Let the appliance preheat for 3 minutes.
7. Open the lid then place patties on the grill plate.
8. Cover the inner pot with an air frying lid. Press start.
9. When the timer reaches 0, then press the cancel button.
10. Serve and enjoy.

Nutritional Value (Amount per Serving):

- Calories 183
- Fat 6.2 g
- Carbohydrates 20.7 g
- Sugar 4.8 g
- Protein 11 g
- Cholesterol 89 mg

Spinach Dip

Preparation Time: 10 minutes
Cooking Time: 20 minutes
Serve: 12

Ingredients:

- 3 oz frozen spinach, defrosted & chopped
- 2 cups mozzarella cheese, shredded
- 8 oz cream cheese
- 1 cup sour cream
- 1 tsp garlic salt

Directions:

1. Add all ingredients into the mixing bowl and mix well.
2. Transfer mixture into the baking dish.
3. Place the inner pot in the PowerXL grill air fryer combo base.
4. Place baking dish into the inner pot.
5. Cover the inner pot with an air frying lid.
6. Select bake mode then set the temperature to 350 F and time for 20 minutes. Press start.
7. When the timer reaches 0, then press the cancel button.
8. Serve and enjoy.

Nutritional Value (Amount per Serving):

- Calories 185
- Fat 16.9 g
- Carbohydrates 2 g
- Sugar 0.3 g
- Protein 7 g
- Cholesterol 49 mg

Healthy Taro Fries

Preparation Time: 10 minutes
Cooking Time: 20 minutes
Serve: 2

Ingredients:

- 8 small taro, peel and cut into fries shape
- 1/4 tsp pepper
- 1 tbsp olive oil
- 1/2 tsp salt

Directions:

1. Add taro fries in a bowl and drizzle with olive oil. Season with pepper and salt.
2. Place the inner pot in the PowerXL grill air fryer combo base.
3. Place grill plate in the inner pot. Cover.
4. Select air fry mode then set the temperature to 350 F and time for 20 minutes. Press start.
5. Let the appliance preheat for 3 minutes.
6. Open the lid then place taro fries on the grill plate.
7. Cover the inner pot with an air frying lid. Press start.
8. When the timer reaches 0, then press the cancel button.
9. Serve and enjoy.

Nutritional Value (Amount per Serving):

- Calories 118
- Fat 7.1 g
- Carbohydrates 13.8 g
- Sugar 0.2 g
- Protein 0.8 g
- Cholesterol 0 mg

Easy Cauliflower Bites

Preparation Time: 10 minutes
Cooking Time: 15 minutes
Serve: 4

Ingredients:

- 1 lb cauliflower florets
- 1 1/2 tsp garlic powder
- 1 tbsp olive oil
- 1 tsp sesame seeds
- 1 tsp ground coriander
- Pepper
- Salt

Directions:

1. Add cauliflower florets and remaining ingredients into the bowl and toss well.
2. Place the inner pot in the PowerXL grill air fryer combo base.
3. Add cauliflower florets into the inner pot.
4. Cover the inner pot with an air frying lid.
5. Select bake mode then set the temperature to 400 F and time for 15 minutes. Press start.
6. When the timer reaches 0, then press the cancel button.
7. Serve and enjoy.

Nutritional Value (Amount per Serving):

- Calories 66
- Fat 4 g
- Carbohydrates 7 g
- Sugar 3 g
- Protein 2.6 g
- Cholesterol 0 mg

Delicious Cheese Dip

Preparation Time: 10 minutes
Cooking Time: 20 minutes
Serve: 8

Ingredients:

- 12 oz goat cheese
- 2 tbsp olive oil
- 1/2 cup parmesan cheese, shredded
- 4 oz cream cheese
- 1 tsp red pepper flakes
- 1 tbsp garlic, minced
- 1/2 tsp salt

Directions:

1. Add all ingredients into the mixing bowl and mix until well combined.
2. Pour mixture into the baking dish.
3. Place the inner pot in the PowerXL grill air fryer combo base.
4. Place baking dish into the inner pot.
5. Cover the inner pot with an air frying lid.
6. Select bake mode then set the temperature to 390 F and time for 20 minutes. Press start.
7. When the timer reaches 0, then press the cancel button.
8. Serve and enjoy.

Nutritional Value (Amount per Serving):

- Calories 295
- Fat 24.9 g
- Carbohydrates 2.3 g
- Sugar 1 g
- Protein 16 g
- Cholesterol 64 mg

Flavorful Chicken Dip

Preparation Time: 10 minutes
Cooking Time: 25 minutes
Serve: 8

Ingredients:

- 2 chicken breasts, cooked and shredded
- 8 oz cream cheese, softened
- 1 cup mozzarella cheese, shredded
- 1 cup cheddar cheese, shredded
- 1/4 cup feta cheese, crumbled
- 1/2 cup ranch dressing
- 1/2 cup hot sauce

Directions:

1. In a mixing bowl, add all ingredients and mix well.
2. Pour bowl mixture into the greased baking dish.
3. Place the inner pot in the PowerXL grill air fryer combo base.
4. Place baking dish into the inner pot.
5. Cover the inner pot with an air frying lid.
6. Select bake mode then set the temperature to 350 F and time for 25 minutes. Press start.
7. When the timer reaches 0, then press the cancel button.
8. Serve and enjoy.

Nutritional Value (Amount per Serving):

- Calories 299
- Fat 23 g
- Carbohydrates 2 g
- Sugar 0.6 g
- Protein 20.8 g
- Cholesterol 94 mg

Healthy Tofu Fries

Preparation Time: 10 minutes
Cooking Time: 40 minutes
Serve: 4

Ingredients:

- 15 oz firm tofu, drained, pressed, and cut into strips
- 2 tbsp olive oil
- 1/4 tsp garlic powder
- 1/4 tsp cayenne
- 1/4 tsp paprika
- 1/2 tsp oregano
- 1/2 tsp basil
- Pepper
- Salt

Directions:

1. Add all ingredients into the mixing bowl and toss well.
2. Place the inner pot in the PowerXL grill air fryer combo base.
3. Place marinated tofu strips into the inner pot.
4. Cover the inner pot with an air frying lid.
5. Select bake mode then set the temperature to 375 F and time for 40 minutes. Press start.
6. Flip tofu strips halfway through.
7. When the timer reaches 0, then press the cancel button.
8. Serve and enjoy.

Nutritional Value (Amount per Serving):

- Calories 137
- Fat 11.5 g
- Carbohydrates 2.3 g
- Sugar 0.8 g
- Protein 8.8 g
- Cholesterol 0 mg

Crispy & Flavorful Okra

Preparation Time: 10 minutes
Cooking Time: 10 minutes
Serve: 2

Ingredients:

- 3 cups okra, wash and dry
- 1 tsp dry mango powder
- 1 tsp fresh lemon juice
- 1 tsp chili powder
- 3 tbsp gram flour
- 1 tsp cumin powder
- Salt

Directions

1. Cut top of okra then makes a deep horizontal cut in each okra and set aside.
2. In a bowl, mix together gram flour, lemon juice, chili powder, cumin powder, mango powder, and salt. Add little water and make a thick batter.
3. Fill the batter in each okra.
4. Place the inner pot in the PowerXL grill air fryer combo base.
5. Place grill plate in the inner pot. Cover.
6. Select air fry mode then set the temperature to 400 F and time for 10 minutes. Press start.
7. Let the appliance preheat for 3 minutes.
8. Open the lid then place okra on the grill plate.
9. Cover the inner pot with an air frying lid. Press start.
10. When the timer reaches 0, then press the cancel button.
11. Serve and enjoy.

Nutritional Value (Amount per Serving):

- Calories 102
- Fat 1.3 g
- Carbohydrates 17.4 g
- Sugar 3.3 g
- Protein 5.2 g
- Cholesterol 0 mg

Spicy Spinach Dip

Preparation Time: 10 minutes
Cooking Time: 30 minutes
Serve: 6

Ingredients:

- 10 oz frozen spinach, thawed and drained
- 1/2 cup onion, diced
- 2 tsp garlic, minced
- 1/2 cup mozzarella cheese, shredded
- 1/2 cup Monterey jack cheese, shredded
- 2 tsp jalapeno pepper, minced
- 1/2 cup cheddar cheese, shredded
- 8 oz cream cheese
- 1/2 tsp salt

Directions:

1. Add all ingredients into the mixing bowl and mix until well combined.
2. Pour mixture into the greased baking dish.
3. Place the inner pot in the PowerXL grill air fryer combo base.
4. Place baking dish into the inner pot.
5. Cover the inner pot with an air frying lid.
6. Select bake mode then set the temperature to 350 F and time for 30 minutes. Press start.
7. When the timer reaches 0, then press the cancel button.
8. Serve and enjoy.

Nutritional Value (Amount per Serving):

- Calories 228
- Fat 19.8 g
- Carbohydrates 4.2 g
- Sugar 0.8 g
- Protein 9.7 g
- Cholesterol 61 mg

Ricotta Dip

Preparation Time: 10 minutes
Cooking Time: 15 minutes
Serve: 6

Ingredients:

- 1 cup ricotta cheese, shredded
- 3/4 cup mozzarella cheese, shredded
- 1 tbsp fresh lime juice
- 2 tbsp olive oil
- 1 tsp garlic, minced
- Pepper
- Salt

Directions:

1. In a bowl, add all ingredients and mix well.
2. Pour bowl mixture into the baking dish.
3. Place the inner pot in the PowerXL grill air fryer combo base.
4. Place baking dish into the inner pot.
5. Cover the inner pot with an air frying lid.
6. Select bake mode then set the temperature to 400 F and time for 15 minutes. Press start.
7. When the timer reaches 0, then press the cancel button.
8. Serve and enjoy.

Nutritional Value (Amount per Serving):

- Calories 121
- Fat 9 g
- Carbohydrates 3 g
- Sugar 0.2 g
- Protein 6 g
- Cholesterol 17 mg

Healthy Carrot Fries

Preparation Time: 10 minutes
Cooking Time: 25 minutes
Serve: 4

Ingredients:

- 4 carrots, peel and cut into fries shape
- 1 tsp cumin powder
- 1/4 tsp chili powder
- 1 1/2 tbsp olive oil
- 1/2 tsp salt

Directions:

1. Add carrots, cumin powder, paprika, oil, and salt into the bowl and toss well.
2. Place the inner pot in the PowerXL grill air fryer combo base.
3. Add carrot fries into the inner pot.
4. Cover the inner pot with an air frying lid.
5. Select bake mode then set the temperature to 450 F and time for 25 minutes. Press start.
6. When the timer reaches 0, then press the cancel button.
7. Serve and enjoy.

Nutritional Value (Amount per Serving):

- Calories 73
- Fat 5.4 g
- Carbohydrates 6.3 g
- Sugar 3 g
- Protein 0.6 g
- Cholesterol 0 mg

Easy Stuffed Mushrooms

Preparation Time: 10 minutes
Cooking Time: 8 minutes
Serve: 4

Ingredients:

- 14 mushrooms, chop stems
- 8 oz cream cheese, softened
- 1/4 cup cheddar cheese, shredded
- 2 oz crab meat, chopped
- 1/2 tsp chili powder
- Pepper
- Salt

Directions:

1. Finely chop mushroom stems.
2. In a bowl, mix cheese, mushroom stems, chili powder, crabmeat, cream cheese, pepper, and salt until well combined.
3. Stuff mushrooms with cheese mixture.
4. Place the inner pot in the PowerXL grill air fryer combo base.
5. Place grill plate in the inner pot. Cover.
6. Select air fry mode then set the temperature to 370 F and time for 8 minutes. Press start.
7. Let the appliance preheat for 3 minutes.
8. Open the lid then place stuffed mushrooms on the grill plate.
9. Cover the inner pot with an air frying lid. Press start.
10. When the timer reaches 0, then press the cancel button.
11. Serve and enjoy.

Nutritional Value (Amount per Serving):

- Calories 254
- Fat 22.6 g
- Carbohydrates 4.1 g
- Sugar 1.3 g
- Protein 9.8 g
- Cholesterol 77 mg

Chicken Stuffed Peppers

Preparation Time: 10 minutes
Cooking Time: 25 minutes
Serve: 12

Ingredients:

- 6 jalapeno peppers, halved
- 1/2 cup chicken, cooked and shredded
- 4 oz cream cheese
- 1/4 cup green onion, sliced
- 1/4 cup Monterey jack cheese, shredded
- 1/4 tsp dried basil
- 1/4 tsp salt

Directions:

1. Mix all ingredients in a bowl except jalapenos.
2. Spoon 1 tablespoon mixture into each jalapeno half.
3. Place the inner pot in the PowerXL grill air fryer combo base.
4. Place stuffed peppers into the inner pot.
5. Cover the inner pot with an air frying lid.
6. Select bake mode then set the temperature to 390 F and time for 25 minutes. Press start.
7. When the timer reaches 0, then press the cancel button.
8. Serve and enjoy.

Nutritional Value (Amount per Serving):

- Calories 54
- Fat 4.2 g
- Carbohydrates 0.9 g
- Sugar 0.3 g
- Protein 3.1 g
- Cholesterol 17 mg

Chapter 9: Desserts

Moist Lemon Cake

Preparation Time: 10 minutes
Cooking Time: 60 minutes
Serve: 10

Ingredients:

- 4 eggs
- 2 tbsp lemon zest
- 1/2 cup fresh lemon juice
- 1/4 cup coconut flour
- 2 cups almond flour
- 1/4 cup erythritol
- 1 tbsp vanilla
- 1/2 cup butter softened
- 2 tsp baking powder

Directions:

1. In a large bowl, whisk all ingredients until a smooth batter is formed.
2. Pour batter into the greased cake pan.
3. Place the inner pot in the PowerXL grill air fryer combo base.
4. Place cake pan into the inner pot.
5. Cover the inner pot with an air frying lid.
6. Select bake mode then set the temperature to 300 F and time for 60 minutes. Press start.
7. When the timer reaches 0, then press the cancel button.
8. Serve and enjoy.

Nutritional Value (Amount per Serving):

- Calories 148
- Fat 13.9 g
- Carbohydrates 8.7 g
- Sugar 6.9 g
- Protein 3.7 g
- Cholesterol 90 mg

Almond Date Brownies

Preparation Time: 10 minutes
Cooking Time: 20 minutes
Serve: 16

Ingredients:

- 1 cup dates, pitted
- 1/2 cup cocoa powder
- 3/4 cup almond flour
- 3/4 cup hot water
- 1 1/2 tsp vanilla
- 3 tbsp honey
- 1/2 tsp baking powder
- Pinch of sea salt

Directions:

1. Add dates and hot water to a bowl and let it sit for 10 minutes.
2. Drain dates and add them into the blender and blend until smooth.
3. Add vanilla, honey, cocoa powder, almond flour, and salt into the blender and blend until smooth.
4. Pour mixture into the greased baking dish.
5. Place the inner pot in the PowerXL grill air fryer combo base.
6. Place baking dish into the inner pot.
7. Cover the inner pot with an air frying lid.
8. Select bake mode then set the temperature to 350 F and time for 20 minutes. Press start.
9. When the timer reaches 0, then press the cancel button.
10. Serve and enjoy.

Nutritional Value (Amount per Serving):

- Calories 58
- Fat 1.1 g
- Carbohydrates 13.5 g
- Sugar 10.4 g
- Protein 1.1 g
- Cholesterol 0 mg

Coconut Carrot Cake

Preparation Time: 10 minutes
Cooking Time: 35 minutes
Serve: 16

Ingredients:

- 2 eggs
- 1/8 tsp ground cloves
- 1 tsp cinnamon
- 1 tsp baking powder
- 2 tbsp shredded coconut
- 1/4 cup pecans, chopped
- 6 tbsp erythritol
- 1/2 tsp vanilla
- 2 tbsp butter, melted
- 1/2 cup carrots, grated
- 3/4 cup almond flour
- Pinch of salt

Directions:

1. In a large bowl, whisk together almond flour, cloves, cinnamon, baking powder, shredded coconut, nuts, sweetener, and salt.
2. Stir in eggs, vanilla, butter, and shredded coconut until well combined.
3. Pour batter into the greased baking dish.
4. Place the inner pot in the PowerXL grill air fryer combo base.
5. Place baking dish into the inner pot.
6. Cover the inner pot with an air frying lid.
7. Select bake mode then set the temperature to 325 F and time for 35 minutes. Press start.
8. When the timer reaches 0, then press the cancel button.
9. Slice and serve.

Nutritional Value (Amount per Serving):

- Calories 59
- Fat 5.5 g
- Carbohydrates 1.6 g
- Sugar 0.5 g
- Protein 1.5 g
- Cholesterol 24 mg

Blueberry Carrot Bars

Preparation Time: 10 minutes
Cooking Time: 30 minutes
Serve: 10

Ingredients:

- 1 egg
- 1/2 cup coconut sugar
- 1/4 cup carrot, shredded
- 1 tsp vanilla
- 1/3 cup Greek yogurt
- 1/2 cup vanilla protein powder
- 1 1/2 cups flour
- 1/2 tbsp cinnamon
- 2 tbsp coconut oil, melted
- 1/3 cup blueberries
- 1/3 cup granola
- 1/3 cup almond flour
- 1/2 tbsp baking powder
- 1 cup milk
- Pinch of salt

Directions:

1. In a mixing bowl, combine together all dry ingredients and flours.
2. In a large bowl, mix together egg, vanilla, coconut oil, milk, and yogurt until smooth.
3. Pour egg mixture into the dry mixture and mix well. Stir in carrots, granola, and blueberries.
4. Pour batter into a greased baking dish and spread evenly.
5. Place the inner pot in the PowerXL grill air fryer combo base.
6. Place baking dish into the inner pot.
7. Cover the inner pot with an air frying lid.
8. Select bake mode then set the temperature to 350 F and time for 30 minutes. Press start.
9. When the timer reaches 0, then press the cancel button.
10. Slice and serve.

Nutritional Value (Amount per Serving):

- Calories 222
- Fat 7.1 g
- Carbohydrates 34.2 g
- Sugar 11.7 g
- Protein 5.5 g
- Cholesterol 24 mg

Yummy Strawberry Cobbler

Preparation Time: 10 minutes
Cooking Time: 45 minutes
Serve: 6

Ingredients:

- 2 cups strawberries, diced
- 1 cup self-rising flour
- 1 1/4 cups sugar
- 1 tsp vanilla
- 1/4 cup butter, melted
- 1 cup milk

Directions:

1. In a bowl, mix together flour and 1 cup sugar. Add milk and whisk until smooth.
2. Add vanilla and butter and mix well.
3. Pour mixture into the greased baking dish and sprinkle with strawberries and top with remaining sugar.
4. Place the inner pot in the PowerXL grill air fryer combo base.
5. Place baking dish into the inner pot.
6. Cover the inner pot with an air frying lid.
7. Select bake mode then set the temperature to 350 F and time for 45 minutes. Press start.
8. When the timer reaches 0, then press the cancel button.
9. Serve and enjoy.

Nutritional Value (Amount per Serving):

- Calories 338
- Fat 8.8 g
- Carbohydrates 63.4 g
- Sugar 46 g
- Protein 3.9 g
- Cholesterol 24 mg

Delicious Peanut Butter Brownie

Preparation Time: 10 minutes
Cooking Time: 20 minutes
Serve: 12

Ingredients:

- 2 eggs
- 1/2 cup peanut butter
- 1/2 tsp baking soda
- 2 tbsp cocoa powder
- 1/4 cup Swerve
- 1/2 cup almond flour
- 2 tsp vanilla
- 1/3 cup coconut oil, melted

Directions:

1. In a bowl, mix together all dry ingredients.
2. Add remaining ingredients to the bowl and mix until well combined.
3. Pour batter into the greased baking dish and spread evenly.
4. Place the inner pot in the PowerXL grill air fryer combo base.
5. Place baking dish in the inner pot.
6. Cover the inner pot with an air frying lid.
7. Select bake mode then set the temperature to 350 F and time for 20 minutes. Press start.
8. When the timer reaches 0, then press the cancel button.
9. Serve and enjoy.

Nutritional Value (Amount per Serving):

- Calories 157
- Fat 14.7 g
- Carbohydrates 3.8 g
- Sugar 1.4 g
- Protein 4.8 g
- Cholesterol 27 mg

Delicious Peanut Butter Cake

Preparation Time: 10 minutes
Cooking Time: 30 minutes
Serve: 8

Ingredients:

- 1 1/2 cups all-purpose flour
- 1/2 cup peanut butter powder
- 1 cup of sugar
- 1 tsp vanilla
- 1/3 cup vegetable oil
- 1 tsp baking soda
- 1 tbsp vinegar
- 1 cup of water
- 1/2 tsp salt

Directions:

1. In a mixing bowl, mix together flour, baking soda, peanut butter powder, sugar, and salt.
2. In a small bowl, whisk together oil, vanilla, vinegar, and water.
3. Pour oil mixture into the flour mixture and stir to combine.
4. Pour batter into the greased baking dish.
5. Place the inner pot in the PowerXL grill air fryer combo base.
6. Place baking dish into the inner pot.
7. Cover the inner pot with an air frying lid.
8. Select bake mode then set the temperature to 350 F and time for 30 minutes. Press start.
9. When the timer reaches 0, then press the cancel button.
10. Slice and serve.

Nutritional Value (Amount per Serving):

- Calories 264
- Fat 9.4 g
- Carbohydrates 43.2 g
- Sugar 25.3 g
- Protein 2.6 g
- Cholesterol 0 mg

Chewy Brownies

Preparation Time: 10 minutes
Cooking Time: 20 minutes
Serve: 16

Ingredients:

- 1 1/3 cups all-purpose flour
- 1/2 tsp baking powder
- 1/3 cup cocoa powder
- 1/2 tsp vanilla
- 1/2 cup vegetable oil
- 1/2 cup water
- 1 cup of sugar
- 1/2 tsp salt

Directions:

1. In a mixing bowl, mix together flour, baking powder, cocoa powder, sugar, and salt.
2. In a small bowl, whisk together oil, water, and vanilla.
3. Pour oil mixture into the flour mixture and mix until combined.
4. Pour batter into the greased baking dish.
5. Place the inner pot in the PowerXL grill air fryer combo base.
6. Place baking dish into the inner pot.
7. Cover the inner pot with an air frying lid.
8. Select bake mode then set the temperature to 350 F and time for 20 minutes. Press start.
9. When the timer reaches 0, then press the cancel button.
10. Slice and serve.

Nutritional Value (Amount per Serving):

- Calories 150
- Fat 7.1 g
- Carbohydrates 21.5 g
- Sugar 12.6 g
- Protein 1.4 g
- Cholesterol 0 mg

Cinnamon Apple Slices

Preparation Time: 10 minutes
Cooking Time: 30 minutes
Serve: 6

Ingredients:

- 5 large sweet apples, cut into 1/4-inch thick slices
- 2 tbsp fresh lemon juice
- 2 tsp cinnamon
- 2 tbsp water

Directions:

1. Add all ingredients to the large bowl and toss until apples are well coated.
2. Transfer apple slices to the baking dish.
3. Place the inner pot in the PowerXL grill air fryer combo base.
4. Place baking dish into the inner pot.
5. Cover the inner pot with an air frying lid.
6. Select bake mode then set the temperature to 350 F and time for 30 minutes. Press start.
7. When the timer reaches 0, then press the cancel button.
8. Serve and enjoy.

Nutritional Value (Amount per Serving):

- Calories 100
- Fat 0.4 g
- Carbohydrates 26.4 g
- Sugar 19.5 g
- Protein 0.6 g
- Cholesterol 0 mg

Simple & Easy Yogurt Cake

Preparation Time: 10 minutes
Cooking Time: 35 minutes
Serve: 12

Ingredients:

- 2 eggs
- 7 oz all-purpose flour
- 2 tsp baking powder
- 8.5 oz yogurt
- 1/4 cup oil
- 7 oz sugar

Directions:

1. In a large bowl, add yogurt, oil, eggs, sugar, flour, and baking powder and mix using a hand mixer until smooth.
2. Pour cake batter into a greased baking dish.
3. Place the inner pot in the PowerXL grill air fryer combo base.
4. Place baking dish into the inner pot.
5. Cover the inner pot with an air frying lid.
6. Select bake mode then set the temperature to 350 F and time for 35 minutes. Press start.
7. When the timer reaches 0, then press the cancel button.
8. Slice and serve.

Nutritional Value (Amount per Serving):

- Calories 188
- Fat 5.7 g
- Carbohydrates 31 g
- Sugar 18.1 g
- Protein 3.8 g
- Cholesterol 28 mg

Chapter 10: 30-Day Meal Plan

Day 1

Breakfast-Delicious Berry Oatmeal

Lunch-Honey Mustard Chicken

Dinner-Healthy Artichoke Casserole

Day 2

Breakfast-Healthy Spinach Frittata

Lunch-Italian Halibut

Dinner-Creamy Cauliflower Casserole

Day 3

Breakfast-Blueberry Oatmeal

Lunch-Chicken with Artichoke Hearts

Dinner-Healthy Broccoli Casserole

Day 4

Breakfast-Almond Butter Oatmeal

Lunch-Delicious Pesto salmon

Dinner-Red Beans Rice

Day 5

Breakfast-Healthy Oat Breakfast Muffins

Lunch-Tender & Juicy Chicken

Dinner-Flavorful Ratatouille

Day 6

Breakfast-Artichoke Mushroom Quiche

Lunch-Salmon Casserole

Dinner-Bean Stew

Day 7

Breakfast-Delicious Jalapeno Bread

Lunch-Roasted Pepper Chicken

Dinner-Barley Risotto

Day 8

Breakfast-Healthy Spinach Frittata

Lunch-Lemon Pepper Basa

Dinner-Mac & Cheese

Day 9

Breakfast-Nutritious Zucchini Muffins

Lunch-Chicken Paillard

Dinner-Tender & Moist Lamb Roast

Day 10

Breakfast-Healthy Kale Zucchini Bake

Lunch-Baked Catfish

Dinner-Italian Pork Roast

Day 11

Breakfast-Delicious Berry Oatmeal

Lunch-Greek Tomato Olive Chicken

Dinner-Pork Chop Cacciatore

Day 12

Breakfast-Healthy Spinach Frittata

Lunch-Lime Cajun Salmon

Dinner-Greek Pork Chops

Day 13

Breakfast-Blueberry Oatmeal

Lunch-Easy Slow cook Chicken

Dinner-Italian Beef Roast

Day 14

Breakfast-Almond Butter Oatmeal

Lunch-Sweet Orange Salmon

Dinner-Juicy Pork Tenderloin

Day 15

Breakfast-Healthy Oat Breakfast Muffins

Lunch-Broccoli Chicken Casserole

Dinner-Dijon Pork Chops

Day 16

Breakfast-Delicious Berry Oatmeal

Lunch-Honey Mustard Chicken

Dinner-Healthy Artichoke Casserole

Day 17

Breakfast-Healthy Spinach Frittata

Lunch-Italian Halibut

Dinner-Creamy Cauliflower Casserole

Day 18

Breakfast-Blueberry Oatmeal

Lunch-Chicken with Artichoke Hearts

Dinner-Healthy Broccoli Casserole

Day 19

Breakfast-Almond Butter Oatmeal

Lunch-Delicious Pesto salmon

Dinner-Red Beans Rice

Day 20

Breakfast-Healthy Oat Breakfast Muffins

Lunch-Tender & Juicy Chicken

Dinner-Flavorful Ratatouille

Day 21

Breakfast-Artichoke Mushroom Quiche

Lunch-Salmon Casserole

Dinner-Bean Stew

Day 22

Breakfast-Delicious Jalapeno Bread

Lunch-Roasted Pepper Chicken

Dinner-Barley Risotto

Day 23

Breakfast-Healthy Spinach Frittata

Lunch-Lemon Pepper Basa

Dinner-Mac & Cheese

Day 24

Breakfast-Nutritious Zucchini Muffins

Lunch-Chicken Paillard

Dinner-Tender & Moist Lamb Roast

Day 25

Breakfast-Healthy Kale Zucchini Bake

Lunch-Baked Catfish

Dinner-Italian Pork Roast

Day 26

Breakfast-Delicious Berry Oatmeal

Lunch-Greek Tomato Olive Chicken

Dinner-Pork Chop Cacciatore

Day 27

Breakfast-Healthy Spinach Frittata

Lunch-Lime Cajun Salmon

Dinner-Greek Pork Chops

Day 28

Breakfast-Blueberry Oatmeal

Lunch-Easy Slow cook Chicken

Dinner-Italian Beef Roast

Day 29

Breakfast-Almond Butter Oatmeal

Lunch-Sweet Orange Salmon

Dinner-Juicy Pork Tenderloin

Day 30

Breakfast-Healthy Oat Breakfast Muffins

Lunch-Broccoli Chicken Casserole

Dinner-Dijon Pork Chops

Conclusion

Keto PowerXL Grill Air Fryer Combo Cookbook amazingly easy recipes to fry, bake, grill, and roast with your Air Fryer! The PowerXL Grill Air Fryer is an easy way to cook delicious healthy meals. Rather than cooking the food in oil and hot fat that may affect your health, the machine uses rapid hot air to circulate around and cook meals. This allows the outside of your food to be crispy and also makes sure that the inside layers are cooked through. PowerXL Grill Air Fryer allows us to cook almost everything and a lot of dishes. We can use the PowerXL Grill Air Fryer to cook Meat, vegetables, poultry, fruit, fish and a wide variety of desserts. Why not grab a copy of this cookbook to delight your friends and family with tasty and healthy meals?

www.ingramcontent.com/pod-product-compliance
Lightning Source LLC
Chambersburg PA
CBHW081400070526
44583CB00020B/2614